MORE THAN MUSIC

MORE THAN MUSIC

CULTURAL STIRRINGS
OF PINK FLOYD'S
THE DARK SIDE OF THE MOON

Lawrence K. English

Algora Publishing
New York

Library of Congress Cataloging-in-Publication Data

Names: English, Lawrence, 1961- author.
Title: More than music: Cultural Stirrings of Pink Floyd's The Dark Side of the Moon /
    Lawrence English.
Description: New York: Algora Publishing, 2021. | Includes bibliographical
    references. | Summary: ""More Than Music" is a rigorous examination of
    Pink Floyd's Dark Side of the Moon, providing clear correlations of the
    music and lyrics to human culture, ancient and present. The songs and
    the album overall evoke and tie together themes from myriad
    philosophical, mythological, psychological, religious, historical,
    literary, and other cultural sources"— Provided by publisher.
Identifiers: LCCN 2020056719 (print) | LCCN 2020056720 (ebook) | ISBN
    9781628944402 (trade paperback) | ISBN 9781628944419 (hardcover) | ISBN
    9781628944426 (pdf)
Subjects: LCSH: Pink Floyd (Musical group). Dark side of the moon. | Rock
    music—1971-1980—History and criticism.
Classification: LCC ML421.P6 E65 2021 (print) | LCC ML421.P6 (ebook) |
    DDC 782.42166092/2—dc23
LC record available at https://lccn.loc.gov/2020056719
LC ebook record available at https://lccn.loc.gov/2020056720

Printed in the United States

To my wife Kimberlee and my son Cameron, who helped me more than they know

TABLE OF CONTENTS

Spiritus Mundi

Jimi Hendrix was dead and the Summer of Love was gone. North Vietnam burned beneath American carpet bombing. Man's giant steps on the moon were growing old. Timothy Leary was already outside, looking in. Richard Nixon was moving from a landslide victory toward a historic disgrace. Charlie Manson got a new home in San Quentin. Bangladesh was starving. The drugs were the best, the music was loud, the Grateful Dead were touring Europe.

Into the tumult of the early 1970s, Pink Floyd released their eighth studio album, *The Dark Side of the Moon.*

1. Shown here is one of the first boot prints left on the Moon, made on July 20, 1969, during the Apollo 11 mission to the Sea of Tranquility. Photo courtesy National Aeronautics and Space Administration.

The Rock Renaissance

On March 1, 2023, *The Dark Side of the Moon* will be fifty years old. *The Dark Side of the Moon* still sells hundreds of copies even now.[1] Being a staple of Classic Rock stations everywhere, you can hear songs from it almost every day, and maybe you can sing along, too, because you have heard the words for years. You find Pink Floyd cover bands selling out in many cities, month after month. You see Pink Floyd prism t-shirts on school kids, their parents, and their grandparents.

What explains the continued fascination of *The Dark Side of the Moon*? Why does it appeal to people who were not around in the Seventies? Why does it appeal to people whose *parents* weren't around in the Seventies?

It is great music, without question. *The Dark Side of the Moon* can be found high on many best-album lists. But the early Seventies was a veritable Classic Rock Renaissance, full of great albums. In 1970 and 1971, all of these superb albums were released:

The Beatles — *Let It Be*
Simon & Garfunkel — *Bridge Over Troubled Water*
Led Zeppelin — *Led Zeppelin III*
Jimi Hendrix — *Band of Gypsys*
Crosby, Stills, Nash & Young — *Déjà Vu*
Deep Purple — *Deep Purple in Rock*
David Bowie — *Hunky Dory* and *The Man Who Sold the World*
The Rolling Stones — *Sticky Fingers*
T. Rex — *Electric Warrior*
The Who — *Who's Next*
Jethro Tull — *Aqualung*
Traffic — *The Low Spark of High Heeled Boys*
Genesis — *Nursery Cryme*
The Doors — *L.A. Woman*

After this incredibly bountiful harvest of music, some pause might have been expected, but things seemed to be accelerating instead: In 1972, Deep Purple released *Machine Head*, a pivotal album in heavy metal history. David Bowie released *The Rise and Fall of Ziggy Stardust and the Spiders From Mars*, moving Glam Rock in new directions. 1972 also saw Bowie working with Mott the Hoople on their *All the Young Dudes* album, another key Glam album. Bowie also worked with Lou Reed on his *Transformer* album, whose

---

[1] Keith Caulfield, "Pink Floyd's 'Dark Side of the Moon' Sales Climb in Wake of Solar Eclipse," *Billboard*. MRC Entertainment, LLC, August 22, 2017. https://www.billboard.com/articles/columns/chart-beat/7940910/pink-floyd-dark-side-of-the-moon-solar-eclipse-sales.

Glam turn might have been a surprise, given his gritty Velvet Underground beginnings. In light of Reed's long and close relationship with Andy Warhol, however, Reed himself did not think it was an enormous change.[2]

A very sophisticated Glam entry came from Roxy Music, debuting with its self-titled work. Roxy Music also introduced Brian Eno into the music world, who would become an ambient music pioneer and a producer of many critically acclaimed albums, including U2's *The Unforgettable Fire*, *How to Dismantle an Atomic Bomb*, *Zooropa*, and *Achtung Baby*; Talking Heads' *More Songs About Buildings and Food*, *Fear of Music*, and *Remain in Light*; John Cale's *Fear*; Devo's *Q: Are We Not Men? A: We Are Devo!*, and *Duty Now For The Future*.

But Rock was exploring many other genres in 1972. The Rolling Stones delivered *Exile on Main St.* Jethro Tull created *Thick as a Brick*. T. Rex turned out *The Slider*, and Yes released *Close to the Edge*. Paul Simon released his self-titled first solo album. Neil Young released his solo *Harvest*. Pete Townshend came out with his solo *Who Came First*. And, as suggested in the introduction, the Grateful Dead released *Europe '72*.

The following year, when *The Dark Side of the Moon* was released, was also full of incredible records. By the time 1973 ended, the air was alive with these new and brilliant releases:

The Who — *Quadrophenia*

Elton John — *Goodbye Yellow Brick Road*

David Bowie — *Aladdin Sane*

Genesis — *Selling England by the Pound*

Led Zeppelin — *Houses of the Holy*

Wings — *Band on the Run*

King Crimson — *Larks' Tongues In Aspic*

Queen — *Queen*

Of course, many, many more albums also came out, but these highlights give some sense of what a fantastically rich musical environment the early 70s were.

The music from these other artists remains great, and songs from many of these groups are still in Classic Rock rotation, but not all of these albums are selling well today. Not all of the covers of these albums are seen on the t-shirts of passers-by, nor is their music played by cover bands. Sometimes, yes, but few are seen as often as you see *The Dark Side of the Moon* t-shirts and Pink Floyd cover bands.

---

[2] Colleen 'Cosmo' Murphy, "The Story of Lou Reed 'Transformer'," Classic Album Sundays (Classic Album Sundays, December 29, 2018), https://classicalbumsundays.com/album-of-the-month-lou-reed-transformer/.

Why You Listen to *The Dark Side of the Moon*

Why does *The Dark Side of the Moon* still speak to people? Why is it that you can listen to it hundreds of times and still not feel you have exhausted it? The reason is that it reverberates on so many levels, as music and myths interplay with the conundrums that humans have engaged with for centuries.

And unlike, for example, Jethro Tull's *Aqualung*, The Who's *Quadrophenia*, or either of David Bowie's *The Rise and Fall of Ziggy Stardust and the Spiders From Mars* or *Aladdin Sane*, *The Dark Side of the Moon* does not revolve around a single theme or a single character. Instead it reaches into many different personae and challenges of life. While *The Dark Side of the Moon* is closely tied to the events of the day and the band's own lives and experiences, it resonates with the deepest foundations of our culture and our selves.

Subtly, meticulously, *The Dark Side of the Moon* taps into themes that frame our lives, and it shows us that we choose whether that frame is a box around us or a window to be climbed through. It makes us question our expectations and assumptions, and coaxes us to pay attention, to really listen, to find out what is being asked of us. From beginning to end, *The Dark Side of The Moon* brings familiar images, symbols, and motifs together in a coherent, deeply moving, integrated message.

Just as the single beam of light enters the prism and exits as a rainbow of color on perhaps the most iconic record cover ever, *The Dark Side of the Moon* illustrates how apparently simple things can contain much more than initially meets the eye.

Track One: Speak to Me

One notable aspect of the album is brought home right from the beginning: Much of what is striking about *The Dark Side of the Moon* is not what most people would call *music* at all — shrieks and hysterical laughter; breathless running; the ticking of too many clocks and a barrage of alarm clocks going off; intimate, confiding voices; airport announcements you cannot quite understand. These sounds and voices are woven in throughout the album, catching your attention with familiar sounds in incongruous places, loosely tying the songs to the world you live in every day, but at the same time setting them apart from it.

The very first thing you hear on the album, in fact, is not music, exactly. The first song on the album, "Speak to Me," begins as drum beats, like a heart, calm and slow. It begins very quietly and gradually grows. It is, you realize, the heartbeat traced on the rainbow electrocardiogram across the inside gatefold of the album. You also notice that the electrocardiogram trace of the heartbeat on the inside cover becomes one of the bands of color in the rainbow on the outside, deepening the imagery that there are connections everywhere, that there is more to things than you may first think.

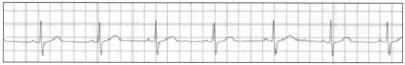

2. The cover of *The Dark Side of The Moon* ties a figurative electrocardiogram trace to an abstract rainbow, connecting the world within to the world

without. Photo is the author's electrocardiogram, taken at the Cleveland Clinic on October 13, 2013.

The heartbeat gradually grows in volume. As it grows louder, though, the sound of a ticking watch begins, then is joined by other sounds that may be more clocks or some kind of machinery. Just as you begin to puzzle over the new sound, trying to place it more precisely, however, your wondering is interrupted by a voice telling you:

> I've been mad for f*ing years, absolutely years. I've been over the edge for yonks. Working me buns off for bands so long. I think, crikey.[3]

And then a different voice tells you:

> I've always been mad, I know I've been mad, like the most of us are. It's very hard to explain why you're a madman, even if you're not a madman.[4]

The first time you heard these voices, you may have actually looked about at others around you, to see if they heard the voices, too. You may have also turned up the volume, in an effort to better make out what they are saying.

3. This July 1973 Pink Floyd concert photograph was taken by Erik Calonious as part of the DOCUMERICA series, the Environmental Protection Agency's program to photographically document subjects of environmental concern. It may be found in the National Archives with Identifier 553890.

---

[3] Kit Rae, "Dark Side of the Moon Bootleg Soundclips and Other Stuff," Dark Side of the Moon Mp3 Soundclips, 2011, http://www.kitrae.net/music/Music_mp3_DSOTM_3.html.
[4] Id.

Behind these oddly unsettling voices, you suddenly hear the ring of a cash register and the rhythmic tear of a cash-register receipt tape. Then you hear footsteps, distinct laughter, and an ominous and growing clatter. As these sounds grow and swirl around each other, a shrieking starts without warning.

Like so many before you, if you had indeed turned up the volume to try to make better sense of the collage of ticking and voices, you now discover that the shrieks have become very, very loud.

Beneath all this bedlam, however, a synthesizer has begun to throb a single note, evocative of the single note that carries the first fifteen seconds of Richard Strauss' 1896 masterpiece "Also sprach Zarathustra" (Thus Spake Zarathustra), a piece that had become popular again around the time *The Dark Side of the Moon* was beginning to be created, because of the 1968 release of Stanley Kubrick's science fiction epic *2001: A Space Odyssey*. It is reported, it should be noted, that Stanley Kubrick had approached Pink Floyd to create the music for his film, but the band declined.[5]

Space itself, of course, was in the air, so to speak. The Apollo space program kept the Moon on the public mind throughout the late 1960s and early 1970s, being a very frequent topic in newspapers and on television. Science fiction books and magazines, TV shows and movies abounded, though some of the most well-recognized TV shows were already in syndication — *Star Trek* stopped making new shows in 1969; *Lost in Space* ended in 1968.

Space was on the radio as well: Songs such as "Space Oddity" (released in 1969), "Life on Mars?" (1971) by David Bowie, and "Rocket Man" by Elton John (1972) were all hits, beautifully capturing personal dimensions of stepping into the void. Remarkably, both "Rocket Man" and "Space Oddity" were produced by the same person, Gus Dudgeon.[6] Dudgeon was an important and innovative British producer who first came to prominence with The Zombies' "She's Not There," and worked closely with Elton John to produce many of his most famous songs, such as "Your Song," "Crocodile Rock," "Daniel," "Goodbye Yellow Brick Road," and "Saturday Night's Alright for Fighting."

"Space Truckin'" rounded out Deep Purple's 1972 *Machine Head*, a hard rock look at future lives in spaceships and on other planets. "Third Stone from the Sun" by Jimi Hendrix (1967) and "2,000 Light Years from Home"

[5] "Pink Floyd," This Day In Music, February 2, 2020, https://www.thisdayinmusic.com/artists/pink-floyd/.

[6] Alexis Petridis, "Obituary: Gus Dudgeon," *The Guardian* (Guardian News and Media, July 23, 2002), https://www.theguardian.com/news/2002/jul/23/guardianobituaries.alexispetridis.

by The Rolling Stones (1967) evoked Pink Floyd's own "Astronomy Domine" and "Interstellar Overdrive" (1967), as well as "Set the Controls for the Heart of the Sun" (1968).

As the shrieking and the machine clatter in "Speak to Me" reaches a crescendo, the sounds of cymbals, guitar and bass abruptly take their place. Cacophonous crescendos are not new to Rock, of course, even chaotic ones. Listen to the bridge in The Beatles' 1967 "A Day In the Life," for example. Spoken sidelights in songs were not novel, either. Think of the words of the captain and sailors in The Beatles' 1966 "Yellow Submarine." But the way the voices speak to you directly, if not always distinctly, in Pink Floyd's "Speak to Me" was certainly novel.

Hearing From the Collective Unconscious

The songwriter Roger Waters has described how he had the idea of using the voices in the segues from song to song. Rather than interview people, he thought of asking them all the same set of questions, which he had written on cards. He gathered whomever would cooperate around the Abbey Road Studios and put them at a podium and recorded their answers to the questions.

Beginning with somewhat benign questions, such as their favorite color, they went on to include the questions prompting the very memorable clips that *The Dark Side of the Moon* is known for, those about insanity, getting into fights, dying, and, finally, the Dark Side of the Moon. Waters sets this scenario out in his own handwriting in a note found in a black envelope labeled "Immersion Questions for Assorted Lunatics," which comes with the sumptuous *The Dark Side of the Moon Immersion Box Set.*[7]

In an interview with *Billboard* magazine celebrating the 1500th week *The Dark Side of the Moon* was on the chart, Waters recalled that the questions that got really good responses were about the last time the person was violent, and whether they thought themselves in the right, and that he found these snippets fit in well with the music.[8]

This novel manner of developing and collecting voice commentaries shows that a critical element of *The Dark Side of the Moon* album was not composed by the musicians at all. Though there appears to be no relationship between these volunteers pressed into action at Abbey Road Studios and the individual album listener at home, there is nonetheless something uncannily

---

[7] Pink Floyd, *The Dark Side of the Moon: Immersion Box Set* (Capitol Records, 2011).
[8] "Roger Waters Revisits The 'Dark Side'." *Billboard.* MRC Entertainment, LLC, May 5, 2006. https://www.billboard.com/articles/news/58519/roger-waters-revisits-the-dark-side.

familiar about these voices. If not actual friends or acquaintances of yours, all the same they seem to be the voices of people whose paths have crossed with yours, snatches of conversations you have overheard somehow.

Thus, from the outset, *The Dark Side of the Moon* has begun to take hold of you in unanticipated ways, ways you cannot readily explain. Of these voices, the founder of analytical psychology, Carl Jung, might have said that by asking these questions of random people, Pink Floyd had tapped into a vein of what he called the Collective Unconscious, a set of common ideas all humans share:[9]

> [J]ust as the human body shows a common anatomy over and above all racial differences, so too, does the psyche possess a common substratum. I have called the latter the collective unconscious. As a common human heritage it transcends all differences of culture and consciousness and does not consist merely of contents capable of becoming conscious, but of latent dispositions toward identical reactions.

The analytical psychology approach developed by Jung differed substantially from the psychoanalytic school led by Sigmund Freud. Jung's approach did not emphasize sexual development to the degree that Freud's did, and included ideas such as the collective unconscious developed and inherited over centuries as having important influences on character and conduct.

Jung theorized that in addition to the conscious mind, the unconscious contained a whole reservoir of psychic tools that had been collected and passed down through hundreds of generations. The consequence of such a collective unconscious is a vast set of shared concepts, characteristics, and tendencies we are all born with. These tools are given to us without regard to what our personal circumstances, surroundings, or experience might be, forming a substructure upon or around which those personal details grow. Jung believed this set of mental patterns was inherited by every human being, influencing their perceptions and reactions at a fundamental level:

> Although we human beings have our own personal life, we are yet in large measure the representatives, the victims and promoters of a collective spirit whose years are counted in centuries.[10]

Jung developed these ideas over years of treating psychiatric patients, which included listening to their stories and dreams. He noticed that people

---

[9] *The Secret of the Golden Flower — A Chinese Book of Life Translated [from the Chinese] and explained by Richard Wilhelm, with a European Commentary by C G. Jung*, trans. Cary F. Baynes (London: Kegan Paul, Trench, Trubner & Co., 1947), 83. Available online as "The Secret Of The Golden Flower By Richard Wilhelm And Carl Jung," March 7, 2013, https://archive.org/details/TheSecretOfTheGoldenFlowerByRichardWilhelmAndCarlJung.

[10] Carl Jung, *Memories, Dreams, Reflections*, revised ed., recorded and edited Aniela Jaffe, trans. Richard and Clara Winston (New York: Random House, 1965), p. 91.

often used images and characters with deep connections to the past — a past to which the individual did not always have direct exposure in his or her own life.

4. Sigmund Freud, G. Stanley Hall, Carl Jung (front row), and Abraham A. Brill, Ernest Jones, Sándor Ferenczi (back row), at Clark University, September 1909. Photo courtesy Library of Congress. https://www.loc.gov/item/92508502/

For example, in his essay "The Personal and the Collective Unconscious," Jung relates how one patient of his described a dream in which her father, who had become a giant, stood on a hill above wheat fields, holding her and rocking her in his arms as the wheat swayed in the wind.[11] After examining this dream in the context of her other dreams for its imagery of God in her father and spirit in the wind for a few paragraphs, Jung observed: [12]

> As my example of the archaic idea of God shows, the unconscious seems to contain other things besides personal acquisitions and belongings. My patient was quite unconscious of the derivation of "spirit" from "wind," or of the parallelism between the two. This content was not the product of her thinking, nor had she ever been taught it. . . . There

---

[11] "C. G. Jung, Collected Works Vol 7 Part 1 The Effects Of The Unconscious Upon Consciousness," Internet Archive, January 1, 1966, https://archive.org/details/C.G.JungCollectedWorksVol7Part1TheEffectsOfTheUnconsciousUponConsciousness/page/n2/mode/1up, p. 132.

[12] *Id.*, pp. 137-38 (italics original, footnote omitted).

is nothing about this image that could be called personal: it is a wholly collective image, the ethnic origin of which has long been known to us. Here is an historical image of world-wide distribution that has come into existence again through natural psychic function. This is not so very surprising, since my patient was born into the world with a human brain which presumably still functions today much as it did of old. We are dealing with a reactivated *archetype*, as I have elsewhere called these primordial images. These images are restored to life by the primitive, analogical mode of thinking peculiar to dreams. It is not a question of inherited ideas, but of inherited thought patterns.

Access to the collective unconscious and its archetypes is not only through dreams, however, and the uncanny familiarity of the voices first heard on "Speak to Me" may reflect its universality and depth.

The idea of an unconscious or subconscious mind at all, much less a collective unconscious, remains an uncomfortable idea for many people despite its being the subject of extensive scientific and philosophical writing for many decades. Though the idea of the unconscious is often popularly associated to Sigmund Freud, William James, for example, discussed both the unconscious and the subconscious dozens of times in his 1890 treatise *The Principles of Psychology*,[13] referring to many, much earlier, discoveries. Despite its currency for over a hundred years, though, the unconscious and subconscious continue to be something questioned or denied outright by many.

It is important to recognize that psychology as a science does progress, albeit in nonlinear fashion. Early efforts to understand patterns are perhaps most admirable for the fact of their recognition that there are indeed patterns in thinking, emotions, and behavior. While subsequent studies may show that this or that portion of a theory is ungrounded, the fact remains that some pattern of some kind had been identified in the evidence that had been collected. That the provisional explanation for the pattern is proven inaccurate does not undermine the recognition of that pattern.

The progress can be likened to the slow evolution of astronomical theories, for example. Before telescopes were used to view the heavens, Copernicus had correctly recognized that the planets revolve around the sun. Using a telescope, Galileo was able to put this heliocentric idea more strongly, and include with it the idea that some of the planets had satellites traveling around them. Another astronomer, Tycho Brahe, who believed that the other planets circled the earth, nonetheless collected an enormous amount of astronomical observations. These records were eventually passed into the hands of Johannes Kepler. Kepler was able to develop mathematical

---

[13] William James, *The Principles of Psychology: William James*, Internet Archive (H. Holt, January 1, 1890), https://archive.org/details/principlespsych04jamegoog/page/n6/mode/2up [Vol. I]; https://archive.org/details/principlespsych0ljamegoog/page/n4/mode/2up [Vol. II].

models, or laws, which showed just how the planets traveled around the sun. Isaac Newton, famous for developing general laws of motion and the theory of gravitation, was able to explain *why* planets obeyed Kepler's laws.

What this shows is that observation and data collection, theory and interpretation often have a complex relationship with one another. While in a general way scientists build upon the work of earlier scientists, they may nonetheless reject out of hand the pieces of an old theory that no longer fit the data.

In the case of the unconscious, this concept may be difficult to accept by some people because they may be unwilling to acknowledge that what we do may not exactly be the product of what we think of as our conscious intentions or current perceptions. As the writer and intellectual Arthur Koestler had put it in *The Ghost in the Machine*, the third book in his trilogy on the human mind:[14]

> Whatever one's philosophical convictions, in everyday life it is impossible to carry on without the implicit belief in personal responsibility; and responsibility implies freedom of choice.

But there is more than just philosophy and argument to support the idea of an unconscious. For example, in a set of experiments performed by Benjamin Libet in 1985, he demonstrated that a person's conscious decision — in these experiments, a simple decision to lift a finger while watching a moving dot on an oscilloscope — is in fact *preceded* by activity in the motor area of the brain.[15,16] That is, that the brain has already begun to direct a motion *before* the person has consciously chosen to move anything.

Subjects of the experiment — of which there were hundreds — were told to watch a dot moving fairly quickly around a numbered circle on an oscilloscope screen. They were also told to lift their finger whenever they had a conscious desire to do so. Finally, they were told to note the position of the moving dot at the time they made their decision.

Thousands of careful measurements showed that the sequence of events was not the expected *decide-to-lift-finger* step followed by a *start-brain-process-to-lift-finger* step followed by a *lift-finger* step. Instead, surprisingly, the *start-brain-process-to-lift-finger* step came 350 milliseconds *before* the *decide-to-lift-finger* step. That is, the subject was not consciously aware of being about to

---

[14] Arthur Koestler, *The Ghost in the Machine* (London: Arkana, 1989), 214.

[15] B. Libet, "Unconscious Cerebral Initiative and the Role of Conscious Will in Voluntary Action," *Behavioral and Brain Sciences*, vol. 8 (New York: Springer, 1995) 529-66, cited and summarized in Daniel M. Wegner and Kurt Gray, *Mind Club — Who Thinks, What Feels, and Why It Matters* (New York: Penguin Putnam Inc., 2016), 304-07.

[16] "Libet Experiments," Libet Experiments (Information Philosopher), accessed September 7, 2020, http://informationphilosopher.com/freedom/libet_experiments.html.

flex a finger when the process began, and only became aware of deciding to flex after the process had begun in their mind.

How this experimental result affects the idea of free will is the subject of often deep and technical dispute. What it unambiguously shows, however, is that there is more to human behavior than the stream of conscious thoughts we may have. Even something as apparently uncomplicated as lifting a finger has more to it than what the conscious mind provides.

Jung's idea of the collective unconscious, based on his own extensive study of his psychiatric patients' dreams, such as the one described above, fairy tales, myths, art, traditional and tribal cultural patterns across the world, was part of the toolkit that supplemented every conscious mind:[17]

> [I]n addition to our immediate consciousness, which is of a thoroughly personal nature and which we believe to be the only empirical psyche (even if we tack on the personal unconscious as an appendix), there exists a second psychic system of a collective, universal, and impersonal nature which is identical in all individuals. This collective unconscious does not develop individually but is inherited. It consists of pre-existent forms, the archetypes, which can only become conscious secondarily and which give definite form to certain psychic contents.

These Jungian archetypes in the collective unconscious are thus the inherited patterns or forms of thought that are an unconscious influence on what we think and do, guiding us at the most fundamental level: "They are, indeed, an instinctive *trend*," Jung said, "as marked as the impulse of birds to build nests, or ants to form organized colonies."[18]

As the British psychiatrist Anthony Stevens observed, archetypes have proven a rich source of scholarly and fanciful writing that strike similar chords across vast geographical boundaries and generations, reflecting their ubiquity in the human mind. Like Charles Darwin, who showed how homologous body structures between species — like the wings of birds and bats, the fins of fish, and the arms of humans — had a shared ancestry, so too Jung saw a common evolutionary origin in symbols and myths. From

---

[17] C. G. Jung, *Collected Works of C. G. Jung: The Archetypes and the Collective Unconscious*, 2nd ed., editors G. Adler, M. Fordham, H. Read, trans. R. F. C. Hull, (London: Routledge & Kegen Paul, 1969), p. 43. Available online as C. G. Jung and R. F. C. Hull, "Collected Works of C. G. Jung : The Archetypes and the Collective Unconscious: C. G. Jung," Internet Archive, December 3, 2012, https://archive.org/details/collectedworksof91cgju/page/n9/mode/2up.

[18] C. G. Jung et al., "Approaching the Unconscious," in *Man and His Symbols* (New York: Dell Pub. Co., 1964), p. 69 (italics original). Available online as "Man and His Symbols : Carl Gustav Jung," Internet Archive, January 1, 1964, https://archive.org/details/B-001-004-443-ALL/page/n65/mode/2up.

this commonality, Jung theorized universal structures in every human mind, reflected in the archetypes.[19]

Jung emphasized that the archetypes were images, forms and substructures that were only given definition and specificity by a person when they encounter something that evokes it. The archetypes have tuned the person in to recognize many aspects of a thing from the start:[20]

> The form of the world into which he is born is already inborn in him as a virtual image. Likewise parents, wife, children, birth and death are inborn in him as virtual images, as psychic aptitudes. These *a priori* categories have by nature a collective character; they are images of parents, wife, and children in general, and are not individual predestinations. We must therefore think of these images as lacking in solid content, hence as unconscious. They only acquire solidity, influence, and eventual consciousness in the encounter with empirical facts, which touch the unconscious aptitude and quicken it to life. They are in a sense the deposits of all our ancestral experiences, but they are not the experiences themselves.

Over the years, Jung and others postulated many, many different archetypes beyond the parents, spouse, children, birth and death mentioned above. Examples of other Jungian archetypes that are familiar from myths and movies are discussed by Jung in his book *Archetypes and the Collective Unconscious*, including:

The Self
Anima and Animus
The Shadow
The Persona
The Wise Old Man
The Hero
The Maiden
The Trickster [21]

Discussion of what each of these archetypes comprises quickly gets very subtle, even arcane: The second edition of his book *The Archetypes and the Collective Unconscious*,[22] published originally in 1959 and then with new material added in 1969, is nearly 420 pages long. While these archetypes will not be discussed further in general, one, the Trickster, will be examined, as it plays an important role in *The Dark Side of the Moon*.

---

[19] Anthony Stevens, *Archetype Revisited: an Updated Natural History of the Self* (London: Brunner-Routledge, 2002), p. 25.

[20] Carl Jung, "C. G. Jung Collected Works Vol 7 Part 2 Individuation," January 1, 1966, https://archive.org/details/C.G.JungCollectedWorksVol7Part2Individuation/page/n9/mode/2u, p. 190.

[21] *Id*.

[22] Jung, *The Archetypes and the Collective Unconscious*.

The Voice of the Trickster

The way the voices first heard on "Speak to Me" (*I've been mad for f*ing years, absolutely years, been over the edge for yonks*) so strongly grab the attention suggests that those voices resonate with one of the archetypes of the collective unconscious. The Trickster seems the most likely choice.

The Trickster is generally described as very direct, even to the point of being thoughtless and rude. As Jung put it in the chapter "On the Psychology of the Trickster-Figure" in *The Archetypes and the Collective Unconscious:* [23]

> In his clearest manifestations he is a faithful reflection of an absolutely undifferentiated human consciousness, corresponding to a psyche that has hardly left the animal level.

Dr. Joseph L. Henderson, whom Jung himself chose to write the "Ancient myths and modern man" chapter in *Man and His Symbols*,[24] described the Trickster as follows:[25]

> Trickster is a figure whose physical appetites dominate his behavior; he has the mentality of an infant. Lacking any purpose beyond the gratification of his primary needs, he is cruel, cynical, and unfeeling. (Our stories of Brer Rabbit or Reynard the Fox preserve the essentials of the Trickster myth.)

The book *Man and His Symbols* was planned, supervised and directed by Jung, and Jung also wrote the keynote chapter, "Approaching the Unconscious." His intent for the book was to present his ideas to the average reader, of reasonable intelligence but with no real knowledge of psychology. It was his final work. As described by John Freeman in the Introduction:[26]

> The last year of his life was devoted almost entirely to this book, and when he died in June 1961, his own section was complete (he finished it, in fact, only some 10 days before his final illness) and his colleagues' chapters had all been approved by him in draft.

Neither Brer Rabbit nor Reynard the Fox may be familiar to many readers today. Brer Rabbit was a trickster figure whose stories originally came from Africa and were popularized in the late 19th century by Joel Chandler Harris, who had become familiar with the folklore of slaves on American plantations. Harris' stories, in turn, were popularized further in the 1946 Disney Company movie *Song of the South*, which is no longer shown in view of its racial characterizations. In these stories, the tiny Brer Rabbit uses his quick

---

[23] *Id.* at p. 260.

[24] Jung, *Man and His Symbols*, p. 11.

[25] Joseph L. Henderson, "Ancient myths and modern man" chapter in Jung, *Man and His Symbols*, p.112.

[26] John Freeman, Introduction, Jung, *Man and His Symbols*, p. 11.

wits to prevail over the much larger characters of Brer Wolf, Brer Bear, and Brer Fox.

5. Photo courtesy The Miriam and Ira D. Wallach Division of Art, Prints and Photographs: Picture Collection, The New York Public Library. "Brer Rabbit turnt 'er aloose, en down she come—ker-swosh!" New York Public Library Digital Collections. Accessed August 22, 2020. http://digitalcollections.nypl. org/items/6bf1c5c5-c460-591e-e040-e00a18062858.

Tracing the European development of the Trickster, Jung said in his *The Archetypes and the Collective Unconscious*:[27]

---

[27] Jung, *The Archetypes and the Collective Unconscious*.

These medieval customs demonstrate the role of the trickster to perfection, and, when they vanished from the precincts of the Church, they appeared again on the profane level of Italian theatricals, as those comic types who, often adorned with enormous ithyphallic emblems, entertained the far from prudish public with ribaldries in true Rabelaisian style. Callot's engravings have preserved these classical figures for posterity—the Pulcinellas, Cucorognas, Chico Sgarras, and the like.

6. This photo of Jacques Callot's etching of a comic performance of the Balli di Sfessania is courtesy Library of Congress, Callot, Jacques, Artist. Balli di Sfessania 'di Jacomo Callot / Jac. Callot, in., fe., [Paris: Jacques Fagnani, 172] https://www.loc.gov/item/90707491/.

Reynard the Fox, on the other hand, lives on in multiple literary forms, first put down in verse centuries ago.[28] Like Brer Rabbit, Reynard overcomes brute strength with cunning. But Reynard was also often portrayed in a way that satirically reflects the contempt of the peasantry for the Church.[29] Versions of Reynard are still found being performed today, with a bit of diligent searching. Brer Rabbit and Reynard the Fox may be seen as stories told by the downtrodden to foster hope.

---

[28] J. J. Mora, "Reynard the Fox," Preface, p. v, Internet Archive (Boston, D. Estes & Co, January 1, 1970), https://archive.org/details/reynardfox00unse/page/n12/mode/1up.
[29] Id.

When the Trickster is identified, it is often a given that the "crazy wisdom," the antics, the flouting of norms, limits, and rules is either (or both) an innate component of the character or a deliberate action chosen by the Trickster. The Trickster has a magnetism that draws others in, whether or not they desire to be drawn in. For example, in the National Book Award winner *The Snow Leopard*, Peter Mattiessen describes the effect of Tukten, one of the Sherpas accompanying his journey to the Himalayas, on those around him, presenting all of the fundamental elements of a Trickster in a living, breathing human being:[30]

> Of his wide experience, Tukten tells tales in that soft voice, and so the other Sherpas listen, but he is not one of them. Ordinarily Tukten would remain among the porters who have taken shelter in a cave down in the canyon, but he is helpful and ingenious, and his mesmerizing voice, coming and going on the wind and rain, seems to fascinate the younger Sherpas, although they are wary of him, and keep their distance. One feels they are afraid of him — not of his violence, though they say he fights when drunk, but of his power. Whatever this man is — wanderer or evil monk, or saint or sorcerer — he seems touched by what Tibetans call the "crazy wisdom": he is free.

But it is not always clear that in the thrall of their own crazy wisdom such Tricksters could actually choose otherwise and conform themselves to norms or expectations. That is, there may be more "crazy" than there is "wisdom," more of Wile E. Coyote than Reynard the Fox. One Navajo Trickster is indeed Coyote, albeit not Wile E. Coyote. As Sallie Nichols described in her book *Jung and Tarot: An Archetypal Journey*:[31]

> Like the Navajo trickster Coyote, the fool is accorded a special role in the social order. His presence serves the ruling powers as a constant reminder that the urge to anarchy exists in human nature and that it must be taken into account.

The Fool in the traditional Tarot deck is often associated with the archetypal Trickster. On the page opposite the illustration of the Fool from the 1916 book *The Illustrated Key to the Tarot: The Veil of Divination*, the author L. W. De Laurence says,

> The conventional explanations say that the Fool signifies the flesh, the sensitive life, and by a peculiar satire its subsidiary name was at one time the alchemist, as depicting folly at the most insensate stage.[32]

---

[30] Peter Matthiessen, *The Snow Leopard* (New York: Bantam Books, 1979), p. 88.

[31] Sallie Nichols, *Jung and Tarot: An Archetypal Journey*, intro. L. van der Post (Boston: Red Wheel/Weiser, LLC, 1980), p. 30.

[32] Lauron William De Laurence, "The Illustrated Key to the Tarot: The Veil of Divination," Internet Archive (Project Gutenberg, August 1, 2018), https://archive.org/details/theillustratedke43548gut, page 81.

7. This illustration from Lauron William De Laurence's *The Illustrated Key to the Tarot: The Veil of Divination*, is courtesy Library of Congress, http://hdl.loc.gov/loc.gdc/scd0001.00020492314.

Elsewhere in her chapter "The Fool in Tarot and in Us," Nichols states,[33]

> [T]he Fool's spontaneous approach to life combines wisdom, madness and folly. When he mixes these ingredients in the right proportions the results are miraculous, but when the mixture curdles, everything can end up a sticky mess.

In the case of Pink Floyd, unfortunately, the latter sticky mess case was exactly the situation: As will be discussed in more detail below in the "Brain

---

[33] *Id.* at p. 24.

Damage" chapter, the Trickster Syd Barrett was the band's first guitarist and initial guiding spirit, to whom many references are made on *The Dark Side of the Moon* and other albums. Barrett, in fact, gave Pink Floyd — The Pink Floyd, as it was at the time — their name.

8. This photo of Syd Barrett's mirrored Fender Esquire guitar, which would have reflected the colored lights that flashed and swirled as the band performed, was taken in 2003 by Francis Pullen, prior to the guitar's inclusion in Pink Floyd's Interstellar exhibition, Cité de la Musique, Paris.

Though an enormously creative force behind the band's early work, Barrett's behavior grew increasingly baffling and bizarre, leading the band to leave him out of later work, including *The Dark Side of the Moon*. Nonetheless, Barrett's embrace of novel, unbounded, psychedelic approaches to music did away with conventions that might otherwise have inhibited Pink Floyd.

Thus, while the mélange of peculiar voices, unusual noises, shrieks, and sound effects in "Speak to Me" make for a disconcerting introductory minute, they do effectively set the stage for a different sort of album, much in the way images shown behind the credits rolling across the screen at the beginning of a movie often give strong hints about the plot and characters you will encounter.

Many Songs, One Album

Every part of *The Dark Side of the Moon* relates to the other parts in a way uncommon for rock albums, making the album a composition to be considered as an artistic whole, rather than as a collection of separate songs. The album moves from one song into the next not seamlessly, exactly, but with transitions that are themselves important to the way you comprehend and internalize the album as a whole. Listening closely, for example, you find that when "Speak to Me" ends, you are already five seconds into the second song, "Breathe."

The album was expressly meant to be a unitary performance, with each song merging into the next to make each album side a single artistic unit. That said, Pink Floyd had not been doctrinaire about albums versus singles: An edited, shorter version of "Money" had been released as a single on May 7, 1973 (with "Any Colour You Like" on the B-side),[34] and a shortened version of "Us and Them" (with "Time" on the B-side) was released as a single on February 4, 1974.[35]

In the case of "Money," the word "bullshit" is edited out.[36] This bowdlerizing of the lyrics was probably critical to its getting airplay, as profanity was not accepted in popular broadcast media at the time. This undoubtedly expanded the exposure "Money" received, and hence boosted the audience which purchased the album with the unedited version.

This is much like the effect of the work of Dr. Thomas Bowdler, who took out such exclamations as "God!" or characters like the prostitute in *Henry IV, Part 2* from Shakespeare's plays to make *The Family Shakespeare*, which a parent could read to a young and impressionable child.[37] While these Bowdler-ized versions of the plays lacked the full impact of Shakespeare's originals, *The*

---

[34] "Pink Floyd: The Official Site," Pink Floyd | The Official Site (Pink Floyd (1987) Limited), accessed September 13, 2020, https://www.pinkfloyd.com/history/timeline_1973.php.

[35] "Pink Floyd: The Official Site," https://www.pinkfloyd.com/history/timeline_1974.php.

[36] "Pink Floyd," This Day In Music, February 2, 2020, https://www.thisdayinmusic.com/artists/pink-floyd/.

[37] Kat Eschner, "The Bowdlers Wanted to Clean Up Shakespeare, Not Become a Byword for Censorship," Smithsonian.com (Smithsonian Institution, July 11, 2017), https://www.smithsonianmag.com/smart-news/bowdlers-wanted-clean-shakespeare-not-become-byword-censorship-180963945.

Family Shakespeare nonetheless introduced Shakespeare's plays to a wider audience than before.[38] Presumably, at least some of these young and impressionable children later pursued the uncensored versions.

When their record label, EMI, allowed individual Pink Floyd songs to be downloaded in March 2010, Pink Floyd sued, inasmuch as their contract stated that tracks cannot be sold unbundled from albums. EMI argued that the contract applied only to physical albums, not downloads. The British courts did not agree, ruling that the label is not entitled to exploit recordings by online distribution or by any other means other than the complete original album, without Pink Floyd's consent.[39]

That consent was eventually agreed upon within a year of the conclusion of the legal proceedings, though with some criticism of the band's prior position with respect to artistic integrity.[40] Nonetheless, and much as in the case of the Bowdlerization of "Money," this step likely expanded the listening audience of the component parts, which likely led to an expanded audience for the total work.

Hence, while versions of several songs from *The Dark Side of the Moon* were indeed released as singles, the unexpurgated songs melting into one another was an important part of what made the album the lasting, integrated masterpiece it is. That integration is illustrated from the outset, as the confusing tumult of "Speak to Me" segues into the structured melody of "Breathe."

Track Two: Breathe

As the crescendo of "Speak to Me" fades, "Breathe" (or "Breathe (In the Air)") bursts forth, imperative and yet hesitant at the same time:

> *Breathe, breathe in the air.*
>
> *Don't be afraid to care.*
>
> *Leave but don't leave me.*
>
> *Look around and choose your own ground.*

---

[38] J. E Luebering, "Thomas Bowdler," *Encyclopædia Britannica* (Encyclopædia Britannica, Inc.), accessed November 22, 2020, https://www.britannica.com/biography/Thomas-Bowdler.

[39] Minara El-Rahman, "The Final Cut: Pink Floyd and EMI Group Lawsuit," Findlaw, March 21, 2019, https://blogs.findlaw.com/decided/2010/03/the-final-cut-pink-floyd-and-emi-group-lawsuit.html.

[40] Sam Jones, "Pink Floyd and EMI Agree Deal Allowing Sale of Single Digital Downloads," *The Guardian* (Guardian News and Media, January 4, 2011), https://www.theguardian.com/music/2011/jan/04/pink-floyd-emi-single-digital-downloads.

The first line urges you to get outside and enjoy the outside air — perhaps to enjoy the bucolic countryside shown on the cover of their 1970 album, *Atom Heart Mother*. But it may also be telling you to become aware of your breathing itself, in the mindfulness sense of Zen Buddhism, such as was becoming popular in the Seventies.

Interest in Zen had been growing in the West, fed by a growing presence of Zen practitioners like the Buddhist monk Thich Nhat Hahn (whom Martin Luther King Jr. nominated for the 1967 Nobel Peace Prize[41]), and publication of popular books like *The Dharma Bums*, by Jack Kerouac, who is best known for his book *On the Road*. Both of these books are still widely read today. (Robert M. Pirsig's *Zen and the Art of Motorcycle Maintenance* was still a couple of years in the future.)

Wherever you find a discussion of Zen, you very quickly find how important breathing is to Zen practice. Some sense of what mindful breathing is and how important it is can be inferred from Shunryu Suzuki's best-selling 1970 book *Zen Mind, Beginner's Mind: Informal Talks on Zen Meditation and Practice*:[42]

> In zazen practice we say your mind should be concentrated on your breathing, but the way to keep your mind on your breathing is to forget all about yourself and just to sit and feel your breathing. If you are concentrated on your breathing you will forget yourself, and if you forget yourself you will be concentrated on your breathing. I do not know which is first. So actually there is no need to try too hard to be concentrated on your breathing. Just do as much as you can. If you continue this practice, eventually you will experience the true existence which comes from emptiness.

Suzuki was the founder of the San Francisco Zen Center and played a profoundly important role in establishing authentic Zen practice in the United States. As one profile described the situation before the San Francisco Zen Center was established:[43]

> Half a century ago, if a person in America was interested in practicing Zen Buddhism, or any kind of Buddhism, there wasn't much they could do other than go to the other side of the world and learn a new language.

---

[41] Brooke Schedneck, "Thich Nhat Hanh, the Buddhist Monk Who Introduced Mindfulness to the West, Prepares to Die," The Conversation, June 4, 2020, https://theconversation.com/thich-nhat-hanh-the-buddhist-monk-who-introduced-mindfulness-to-the-west-prepares-to-die-111142.

[42] Shunryu Suzuki, *Zen Mind, Beginner's Mind: Informal Talks on Zen Meditation and Practice, 40th Anniversary* (Boston: Shambhala, 2010), p. 103.

[43] David R Chadwick, "A Profile of the San Francisco Zen Center," Crooked Cucumber, April 2002, http://www.cuke.com/dchad/writ/short/sfzc%20profile.html.

The path to emptiness through concentration on breathing requires the quieting of the chatter that so often clouds the mind, so that you might stop, as Suzuki put it, "wandering around the goal with your monkey mind."[44]

Although the rhyming couplet of *Breathe, breathe in the air/Don't be afraid to care* could be such a call to mindfulness, it is immediately offset by the more secular entreaty, *Leave but don't leave me.* This sentence seems a fragment of dialogue between a two people discussing the path they would take together if they could, as opposed to being part of an internal monologue, as the first lines appeared to be.

Whether the two people talking could be called a couple is debatable, though, as there is no real romance to be found on *The Dark Side of the Moon.* Despite its profound breadth and depth, love between two people is simply not one of the areas that the album explores. Even if one did assume that it is a couple's dialogue, moreover, there is little else in the balance of the album to give color or context to a couple's relationship. A few more colloquies do occur within the album, but those are also somewhat ambiguous.

Looking into Pink Floyd's other work, the phrase could be a continuation of the words between the two people introduced in the song "Fearless," from the 1971 *Meddle* album. Here again, though, these seem to be two people who are indeed on intimate, and yet not necessarily romantic, terms:

> You say the hill's too steep to climb, chiding.
>
> You say you'd like to see me try, climbing.
>
> You pick the place and I'll choose the time
>
> And I'll climb the hill in my own way.
>
> Just wait a while for the right day,
>
> And as I rise above the tree-line and the clouds
>
> I look down, hear the sound of the things you said today[45]

In "Fearless," the speaker is asserting his or her independence despite the doubts or discouragement of the second person. In "Breathe," in contrast, it appears to be one person encouraging another toward independence and autonomy — just so long as the other does not become so independent that the two are no longer close. The dialogue in each song is earnest, reflecting important choices to be made at that time.

"Breathe" goes on, however, to contend that the choices you make become the path that is your life. The opportunity to choose is, therefore, something very much to be seized, as there is nothing else:

---

[44] Suzuki, *Zen Mind, Beginner's Mind*, p. 119.
[45] Pink Floyd, "Fearless Lyrics," Fearless lyrics — Meddle Lyrics — Pink Floyd Lyrics, November 2020, http://www.pink-floyd-lyrics.com/html/fearless-meddle-lyrics.html.

Look around and choose your own ground.

Long you live and high you fly

And smiles you'll give and tears you'll cry

And all you touch and all you see

Is all your life will ever be.

There is a tension between the seemingly upbeat notion of a long, high-flying life, full of laughter and tears, and the cold finality of it being the sum of life's meaning. But "Breathe" is unequivocal in its assertion that outside of what you choose, there is nothing. It is a flat, unsentimental description of what can actually be experienced by human beings, whether or not one believes there is something that comes after. That is, whether or not there is something after is not something the living can empirically observe in any verifiable way. Whether or not it is believed, which is a matter of faith, it cannot be known.

Kierkegaard and Finality, Updike and Fecklessness

The idea that your life is composed only of what you make it is not neces-sarily a *per se* rejection of an afterlife, however. For example, the nineteenth century Danish philosopher Søren Kierkegaard ardently believed in a Chris-tian eternity, but just as strongly believed that one's place in it was abso-lutely determined by the choices you made during that life, period. As he observed in 1845:[46]

> When death comes, it makes [a] pronouncement, "Thus far, not one step farther." Then it is finished, and not a letter may be added; the meaning is complete, not another sound is to be heard — it is over. If it is impossible to combine all the pronouncements about life made by the innumerable hosts of the living, the dead all unite in a single pronouncement, in one single word to the living— "Stand still!" If it is impossible to unite all the pronouncements of the innumerable hosts of the living about their striving in life, all the dead unite in saying one single thing, "Now it is over."

Notwithstanding Kierkegaard's unyielding belief in the importance of faith, he is known as the father of existentialism,[47] a philosophy that many consider as rejecting faith as a valid basis for an authentic life. This apparent paradox is resolved in the sense that Kierkegaard laid the foundation for

---

[46] Søren Kierkegaard, "Three Discourses On Imagined Occasions," Internet Archive (Digital Library of India, January 1, 1970), https://archive.org/details/in.ernet.dli.2015.504972/page/n99/mode/2up, p. 85.

[47] William McDonald, "Søren Kierkegaard," *Stanford Encyclopedia of Philosophy* (Stanford University, November 10, 2017), https://plato.stanford.edu/entries/kierkegaard/.

modern existentialism in his insistence that personal choice during life is the absolute determiner of the ultimate meaning of that life.

This fierce insistence on the personal was expressed in such works as *Attack upon 'Christendom,'* in which he excoriated the establishment church of his day as something Jesus Christ would not have recognized or accepted as consistent with His teaching. Kierkegaard's last work, it retains Kierkegaard's biting wit. In an essay memorably entitled, "That we ("Christendom") cannot in any wise appropriate Christ's promises to ourselves, for we are not in the place where Christ and the New Testament require one to be in order to be a Christian," Kierkegaard writes:[48]

> Imagine that there was a mighty spirit who had promised to certain men his protection, but upon the condition that they should make their appearance at a definite place where it was dangerous to go. Suppose that these men forbore to make their appearance at that definite place, but went home to their parlors and talked to one another in enthusiastic terms about how this spirit had promised them his potent protection, so that no one should be able to harm them. Is not this ridiculous?

> So it is with "Christendom." Christianity and the New Testament understood something perfectly definite by believing; to believe is to venture out as decisively as it is possible for a man to do, breaking with everything a man naturally loves, breaking, in order to save his own soul, with that in which he naturally has his life. But to him who believes is promised also assistance against all danger.

> But in "Christendom" we play at believing, play at being Christians; as far as possible from any breach with what we love, we remain at home, in the parlor, in the old grooves of finiteness — and then we go and twaddle with one another, or let the priest twaddle to us, about all the promises which are found in the New Testament, that no one shall harm us, that the gates of hell shall not prevail against us, against the Church, etc."

In *Fear and Trembling*,[49] moreover, his most well-known work, Kierkegaard examines closely the biblical story of Abraham, who had been told by God to sacrifice his son Isaac. God did not explain why he should do this, but Abraham's faith was so strong that he had gotten to the point of raising a knife over Isaac, before an angel interceded. Abraham had not expected or counted on such an intercession, nor did he understand what would be accomplished

---

[48] Søren Kierkegaard, *Kierkegaard's Attack upon "Christendom": 1848–1855*, trans. Walter Lowrie (Boston: The Beacon Press, 1960), p. 191. This may be found online at Søren Kierkegaard, "Kierkegaard's Attack upon "Christendom," 1854–185" (University of Florida, March 3, 2011), https://archive.org/stream/kierkegaardsatta00kier.

[49] Søren Kierkegaard, "Fear-and-Trembling-Johannes-De-Silentio," trans. Walter Lowrie, Internet Archive (Siegfried, July 5, 2015), https://archive.org/details/fear-and-trembling-johannes-de-silentio.

by this sacrifice; Abraham only knew what God had instructed him to do. This, to Kierkegaard, was what was necessary to choose real faith: an utter surrender of everything he would love more than God.

Such an uncompromising attitude is emblematic of existentialism. That Kierkegaard's attitude is an uncompromising embrace of an external source of meaning — faith in God — makes it a complicated idea in existential thought. As will be discussed in the context of "Eclipse," Jean-Paul Sartre used this same Biblical story centuries later to show that it is the individual who decides whose voice he or she hears, and that it is only the individual who can choose what is right or wrong.

Whether or not there is something after life, there is nonetheless the life to be led while you are living. Hard on the heels of the pronouncement in verse two of "Breathe" that your life is exactly and only what you make it comes the equally unsentimental reminder in the third verse that to live a life of any sort, one must make a living:

Run, rabbit run.

Dig that hole, forget the sun,

And when at last the work is done

Don't sit down it's time to dig another one.

These lines view making a living from a distinctly working-class perspective, which views work as a necessity, as opposed to some fulfilling, elective vocation. As do rabbits, however, coal miners need holes to survive, and you cannot simply *Look around and choose your own ground* without being able to pay to acquire it and continue to pay to maintain it.

This subterranean motif may reflect the background of the songwriter, Roger Waters: Waters' grandfather was a coal miner and Labour Party activist,[50] and he may well have served as the germination point of these lines. As discussed later, Waters also took much inspiration for many songs, though in an embittered way, from his father.

---

[50] Cole Moreton, "Roger Waters: Backstage as He Prepares for The Wall Live Show," Daily Mail Online (Associated Newspapers, November 7, 2010), https://www.dailymail.co.uk/home/moslive/article-1327045/Roger-Waters-Backstage-prepares-The-Wall-live-show.html.

9. This photograph of the 1495 woodcut illustrating *The angel of the Lord preventing Abraham from sacrificing Isaac on the Rock Moriah* is courtesy Library of Congress Rare Book and Special Collections Division, https://www.loc.gov/item/2007681127/.

Note that in 1960, John Updike had written *Rabbit, Run*, a novel chronicling a few months in the life of a character named Harry Angstrom, whose nickname was Rabbit. It follows Angstrom as he copes somewhat poorly with his life as a suburban salesman of a small kitchen gadget, and whose best days seem to have been as a high school basketball star. (Bruce Springsteen's song of peaking in high school, "Glory Days," was as yet many years in the future.) With a variety of loveless yet explicitly sexual episodes, Rabbit tries to fill a void, but does not transcend his unhappy, nostalgic stagnation.

Rabbit, Run may have been recalled to Pink Floyd's attention in 1971, when was followed by the sequel, *Rabbit Redux*. In *Rabbit Redux*, Angstrom is facing middle age as an operator at a printing plant whose wife has left him with a 13-year-old. The 1960s issues of drugs, race, sex, and politics are a rich background to Angstrom's journey from establishing his own commune to ultimately reuniting with his wife and returning to an ordinary, pedestrian life.

It is not clear that the earlier *Rabbit, Run* or the more album-contemporary *Rabbit Redux* were an influence on the creation of *The Dark Side of The Moon* generally or the lyrics of "Breathe" specifically. These *Rabbit* novels do, however, resonate with two disconsolate background themes of the 1960s and 70s, of how a life can unravel and even decay if not honestly and consistently attended to, and that activity and distraction are not the same as fulfillment and satisfaction.

Camus, Sartre, and Laboring

In their differing ways of reflecting how what you do with your days is the sum of your life, the second and third verse of "Breathe" are closely related. This may be a dismal thought to someone whose work is tied to actual mining, manufacturing, or some other industrial piecework process, or in some repetitive administrative or sales position. Between the machines or desk at which one toils and the time-clock that measures the days, it is trading a long week of work for a short weekend break, followed by yet another week of just the same.

This is close to the observation in Albert Camus' first essay in his 1955 collection, *The Myth of Sisyphus and Other Essays*, "An Absurd Reasoning:"[51]

> Rising, streetcar, four hours in the office or the factory, meal, streetcar, four hours of work, meal, sleep, and Monday Tuesday Wednesday Thursday Friday and Saturday according to the same rhythm—this path is easily followed most of the time. But one day the "why" arises and everything begins in that weariness tinged with amazement.

Albert Camus had been many things — journalist, editor, playwright, novelist, political activist — but denied being a philosopher, however philo-

---

[51] Albert Camus, "'An Absurd Reasoning,'" in *The Myth of Sisyphus and Other Essays*, trans. Justin O'Brien (New York: Vintage Books, 1955), p. 10.

sophical his writings might be.[52] Camus, most well-known for his novel *The Stranger*, won the Nobel Prize for Literature in 1957.[53]

10. Camus is shown in this photo by Jan Ehnemark on December 10, 1957, in conversation with two women at the party after he was awarded the 1957 Nobel Prize for Literature. Photo number SvD 31308, courtesy Stockholm City Museum.

The Stranger introduced many readers to a character who did not respond to significant events — his mother's death, his own trial for murder, for example — as expected, and who was entirely unapologetic for his behavior. This short novel was a good introduction to Camus' sense that the universe was itself indifferent to individuals, but left out how much joy and beauty Camus believed the world had to offer as it was. Joy, as most people define it, is not to be found in *The Stranger*.

---

[52] Ronald Aronson, "Albert Camus," *Stanford Encyclopedia of Philosophy* (Stanford University, April 10, 2017), https://plato.stanford.edu/entries/camus/.
[53] "Albert Camus Facts," NobelPrize.org (Nobel Media AB), accessed November 22, 2020, https://www.nobelprize.org/prizes/literature/1957/camus/facts/.

Camus had been friends with Jean-Paul Sartre, the most famous and influential existentialist, and, in consequence, Camus was also labeled an existentialist. Camus did not accept that designation, either. Camus and Sartre eventually had a public falling out over the differences in their views.

This difference may be characterized in a simplified way as Sartre maintaining that a person constructs his entire identity, without any external constraint or compulsion. Camus believed that although humans' place in the universe was absurd and that no meaning intrinsically accompanied it, happiness could still be found in the recognition that one is master of one's own fate. Camus also believed, however, that there were indeed certain intrinsic rules to existence, such as that violence is always wrong. Their philosophical differences were compounded by political differences, and the two wound up publicly saying quite unpleasant things about one another.[54]

Just as Camus had received the Nobel Prize for Literature in 1957, Jean-Paul Sartre had been awarded the same in 1964, but famously would not accept it. As the front-page headline in the *New York Times* on October 23, 1964 put it: "Sartre Awarded Nobel Prize, but Rejects It; Existentialist Thinks His Writings Would Be Compromised; $53,000 Will Revert to Fund, Swedish Academy Says."[55] Sartre apologized publicly for any appearance of scandal for his rejection of the prize, but explained that he did not accept any awards and did not want it to impact his writing.[56]

The Swedish Academy, which keeps its nomination and selection proceedings secret for fifty years, eventually disclosed that Sartre had in fact told them more than a week before — by letter of October 14 — that he would decline the prize were it offered to him.[57] The Academy made the award nonetheless, and Sartre turned it down, just as he said.[58]

This renunciation of the Nobel Prize gives an intimation of Sartre's rigorous approach to life, beginning with his own, a rigor we had already

[54] Greg Stone, "Why Camus Was Not An Existentialist," *Philosophy Now: a magazine of ideas* (Philosophy Now, 2016), https://philosophynow.org/issues/115/Why_Camus_Was_Not_An_Existentialist.

[55] "Sartre Awarded Nobel Prize, but Rejects It; Existentialist Thinks His Writings Would. Be Compromised; $53,000 Will Revert to Fund, Swedish Academy Says," *The New York Times* (The New York Times Company, October 23, 1964), https://www.nytimes.com/1964/10/23/archives/sartre-awarded-nobel-prize-but-rejects-it-existentialist-thinks-his.html.

[56] "Jean-Paul Sartre — Documentary," NobelPrize.org (Nobel Media AB), accessed September 19, 2020, https://www.nobelprize.org/prizes/literature/1964/sartre/documentary/.

[57] Alison Flood, "Jean-Paul Sartre Rejected Nobel Prize in a Letter to Jury That Arrived Too Late," *The Guardian* (Guardian News and Media, January 5, 2015), https://www.theguardian.com/books/2015/jan/05/sartre-nobel-prize-literature-letter-swedish-academy.

[58] *Id.*

seen with Kierkegaard. Sartre strongly believed that nothing outside a person determines the meaning of a life, but that each person was completely free to determine its meaning. Sartre had developed these views through his military service and time as a prisoner of war, journalist, playwright, novelist, and essayist.

Sartre also believed that for labor to have meaning, it must be part of a person's projection into the future of what he or she desires to become. He is uncompromising in his view that it is the individual her- or himself who determines what they "should" do, not some set of principles laid down by others.

This is aptly illustrated by an anecdote in *Existentialism and Humanism*, in which a student came to him during World War II. The student's mother was living with him after his father showed himself to be a collaborator, and his brother had been killed in battle by the Germans. The student had to choose between going to England to join the Free French Forces or caring for his mother. The student arrived at the judgment that he should go with the choice that his feelings drove him toward.[59] Sartre observed that the student's choice to discuss this with Sartre, as opposed to a priest with collaborationist views or a priest with resistance views, determined what kind of advice he wanted to hear:[60]

> Similarly, in coming to me, he knew what advice I should give him, and I had but one reply to make. You are free, therefore choose — that is to say, invent. No rule of general morality can show you what you ought to do: no signs are vouchsafed in this world.

Sartre often dramatized his views through the fictional characters in his stories, novels, and plays. The depth of his view of meaningful work, for example, is intimated by the character Mathieu Delarue in *The Age of Reason*, the first novel in his trilogy *Roads to Freedom*. Mathieu is a philosophy teacher, and is speaking at an exhibit of the works of Paul Gauguin with Ivich Serguine, a young student whose father was from an aristocratic family:[61]

> "That's the man who — went away, isn't it?" asked Ivich suddenly.

> "Yes," said Mathieu eagerly. "Would you like me to tell you the story of his life?"

> "I think I know it: he was married, and he had children — isn't that so?"

---

[59] Jean-Paul Sartre, *Existentialism and Humanism*, tr. and introd. Philip Mairet (London: Methuen, 1948), pp. 35-36.

[60] *Id.*, at p. 38.

[61] Jean-Paul Sartre, *The Age of Reason*, trans. Eric Sutton (New York: Random House, 1947), p. 97.

"Yes. He had a job in a bank. And on Sunday he used to go out into the suburbs with an easel and a box of colors. He was what was called a Sunday painter."

"A Sunday painter?"

"Yes, that's what he was to begin with — it means an amateur who messes about with paints and canvases on Sunday; just as people take a rod and line and go out fishing. Partly for health reasons, too — painting landscapes gets a man out into the country, and good air."

Ivich began to laugh, but not with the expression that Mathieu expected.

"I suppose you think it funny that he should have begun as a Sunday painter," asked Mathieu uneasily.

"It wasn't him I was thinking about."

"What was it, then?"

"I was wondering whether people ever talked about Sunday writers, too."

Sunday writers: those petty bourgeois who wrote a short story or five or six poems every year to inject a little idealism into their lives. For health reasons. Mathieu shuddered.

In "Breathe," however, it does not appear that the work in which the subject of the song is engaged is something intrinsically meaningful to him or her, or reflect the values toward which they would project themselves. It thus does not seem that either Camus or Sartre would heartily endorse it.

Blake as Visionary, Lawrence as Witness

The idea that repetitive industrial work may lack intrinsic meaning has been a common theme in the arts since the dawn of the Industrial Revolution. As early as 1810, the visionary poet William Blake was already moved to write how factories — *dark Satanic Mills* — had begun to corrupt England. Imagining what Jesus might have encountered during his legendary visit to England, Blake wrote:[62]

And did those feet in ancient time

Walk upon England's mountains green?

And was the holy Lamb of God

On England's pleasant pastures seen?

---

[62] William Blake, "Poetry And Prose Of William Blake," ed. Geoffrey Keynes, Internet Archive (The Nonesuch Press, Bloomsbury, November 2, 2018), https://archive.org/details/dli.bengal.10689.21604.

> And did the Countenance Divine
>
> Shine forth upon our clouded hills?
>
> And was Jerusalem builded here
>
> Among these dark Satanic Mills?

Blake could see that mechanization was changing the face of England. By 1810, when "And did those feet in ancient time" was published, the steam engine had been improved to do much more than pump water out of mines. It was powering new kinds of industrial machinery, and the power loom for weaving cloth on a large scale had gone into wide use.[63]

The combination of technological innovations and steeply increased demand fostered enormous growth in mining, with the amount of coal mined swelling by a factor of 25 times from 1800 to 1900. In 1913, the writer D.H. Lawrence, the son of a miner, most well known as the author of *Lady Chatterley's Lover*, placed coal miners — colliers — amidst idyllic country scenes in his realistic autobiographical novel *Sons and Lovers*:[64]

> Then he looked wistfully out of the window. Already he was a prisoner of industrialism. Large sunflowers stared over the old red wall of the garden opposite, looking in their jolly way down on the women who were hurrying with something for dinner. The valley was full of corn, brightening in the sun. Two colliers, among the fields, waved their small white plumes of steam. Far off on the hills were the woods of Annesley, dark and fascinating. Already his heart went down. He was being taken into bondage. His freedom in the beloved home valley was going now.

While famous (or infamous) for its descriptions of relations between the sexes, Lawrence's *Lady Chatterley's Lover*, published in 1928, contained memorably vivid descriptions of the gloom which accompanied industrialization. For example:[65]

> With the stoicism of the young she took in the utter, soulless ugliness of the coal-and-iron Midlands at a glance, and left it at what it was: unbelievable and not to be thought about.
>
> . . .

---

[63] History.com Editors, "Industrial Revolution," History.com (A&E Television Networks, September 9, 2019), https://www.history.com/topics/industrial-revolution/industrial-revolution.

[64] D. H. Lawrence, "Sons and Lovers," Internet Archive Moulin Digital Editions (Mitchell Kennerley, New York, January 1, 1970), https://archive.org/details/lawrence_d_h_1885_1930_sons_and_lovers, p. 77.

[65] D. H. Lawrence, "Lady Chatterley's Lover," Internet Archive (Digital Library of India Item 2015.38592, January 1, 1970), https://archive.org/details/in.ernet.dli.2015.38592, pp. 19-20 163, 173, 182.

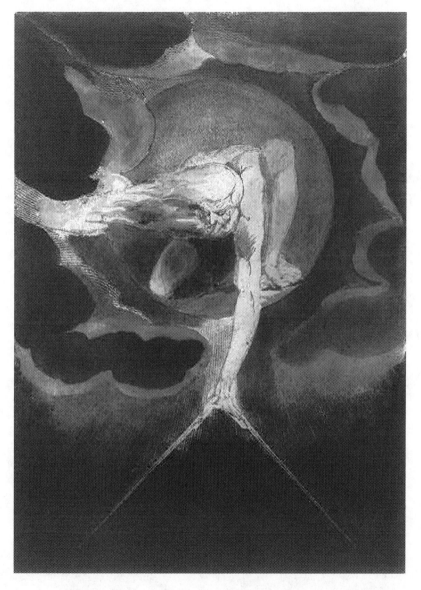

11. In William Blake's 1794 metal relief etching "Ancient of days" — frontispiece of *Europe a Prophecy* — his mythical creature Urizen measures out the material world. This photograph is courtesy the Library of Congress Rosenwald Collection, https://www.loc.gov/item/2005689083/.

Tevershall pit-bank was burning, had been burning for years, and it would cost thousands to put it out. So it had to burn. And when the wind was that way, which was often, the house was full of the stench of this sulphurous combustion of the earth's excrement. But even on windless days the air always smelt of something under-earth: sulphur, iron, coal, or acid. And even on the Christmas roses the smuts settled persistently, incredible, like black manna from the skies of doom.

. . .

It was a world of iron and coal, the cruelty of iron and the smoke of coal, and the endless, endless greed that drove it all. Only greed, greed stirring in its sleep.

. . .

The car ploughed uphill through the long squalid straggle of Tevershall, the blackened brick dwellings, the black slate roofs glistening their sharp edges, the mud black with coal-dust, the pavements wet and black. It was as if dismalness had soaked through and through everything. The utter negation of natural beauty, the utter negation of the gladness of life, the utter absence of the instinct for shapely beauty which every bird and beast has, the utter death of the human intuitive faculty was appalling.

. . .

The iron and the coal had eaten deep into the bodies and souls of the men.

This novel had been thrust back into widespread attention in 1960 by the landmark acquittal of its publisher, Penguin Books, of obscenity charges, buoyed by the literary merit of passages such as those above.[66] Such passages resonate strongly with the *Run, rabbit run* tenor of "Time," being set in actual coal country.

Moving Images

The dismal effects of Industrialism were certainly not exclusive to mining, of course. Factories of all kinds were becoming commonplace. The image of being trapped by factory shift work became widespread in film, as well. Whether you watch Fritz Lang's 1927 *Metropolis* or Charlie Chaplin's 1936 *Modern Times*, for example, there are inescapable images of the individual reacting to machinery or serving an assembly line that moves along according to the line's own clockwork without regard to any human feeling.

---

[66]Geoffrey Robertson, "The Trial of Lady Chatterley's Lover," *The Guardian* (Guardian News and Media, October 22, 2010), https://www.theguardian.com/books/2010/oct/22/dh-lawrence-lady-chatterley-trial.

12. Fritz Lang's 1927 classic *Metropolis* provided powerful images of how industry could become a trap for those who worked in factories. Photo courtesy BreveStoriaDelCinema.org.

Though it may be more than another generation since *The Dark Side of the Moon* was produced, which itself was more than a generation after *Metropolis* or *Modern Times*, today's factory assembly lines are broadly associated with enormous strides in reduced or more-flexible hours, improved benefits, and safer, cleaner working conditions, more inclusive team concepts in management and decision-making, and greater employee recognition. There may also be assistance by robotics or even artificial intelligence, making manufacturing more mentally stimulating as it makes it less physically demanding.

But the underlying relation of the worker serving production and/or the machinery thereof remains, though often with subtle and ironic twists. For example, touting the fact that workers may gain exposure to and experience with high technology in supporting advanced manufacturing processes can be more cynically viewed as merely tending a more sophisticated machine.

And when at last the work is done,

Don't sit down, it's time to dig another one.

13. Charlie Chaplin's 1936 *Modern Times* takes an average person, The Tramp, from factory to insane asylum and then jail. This publicity shot is courtesy United Artists.

There is another way to view manufacturing, however. While it was not something that could have influenced the development of *The Dark Side of the Moon*, Michael Moore's 1989 film *Roger and Me* illustrated another aspect of industrialization.

The movie chronicles the devastation of Flint, Michigan, following the closure of eleven General Motors automotive factories to move them to Mexico, resulting in the laying off of 30,000 GM workers.[67] Through individual anecdotes of how the plant closures affected them, a clear picture is created of the loss of camaraderie and community that had been fostered around and in the factories. Thus, the film illustrates how the work of major manufacturing cannot be viewed in the abstract, but that the environment it helps foster allows meaning to be cultivated. That is, the meaning of work on an assembly line cannot be determined standing alone, but must be considered as a part of the whole situation the workers themselves create.

Comparing the factories of Flint, Michigan, when they were open, to the coal mines in the British Midlands, however, shows that heavy physical labor does not by itself create a positive community spirit. It is, in a sense, the flip side of the scene from Jean-Paul Sartre's play *No Exit* in which one of the characters famously exclaims that Hell is other people. (*No Exit* is discussed further, in the context of the song "Time.") As shown by the sense of community that had been lost in Flint, a sort of Heaven can have been made of other

[67] "Roger & Me (1989) — Plot Summary," IMDb (IMDb.com), accessed September 26, 2020, https://www.imdb.com/title/tt0098213/plotsummary?ref_=tt_stry_pl.

people. It is what people make of their circumstances, as opposed to the circumstances standing alone that matters.

Since this verse in "Breathe" reminding the listener of how an entire class of society lives comes on the heels of the first two, more personal, private, verses, this picture of repetitive work could be interpreted as motivation to seek a better job or even pursue a calling. When "Breathe" does return to the image of a high life in the last verse, however, it suggests that your entertainment and excitement come at a cost, and that the pursuit of the high life in fact keeps you from seeking higher things.

"Breathe" also seems to say that although the achievement of the high life is not a given, it is not necessarily a good thing if it is finally acquired:

> For long you live and high you fly,
>
> But only if you ride the tide,
>
> And balanced on the biggest wave
>
> You race towards an early grave.

The moderately encouraging voice from the second verse is thus tempered by the illustration in the fourth verse; that is, while *all you touch and all you see [i]s all your life will ever be*, each thing you choose to touch or see necessarily excludes other choices (*But only if you ride the tide*), and may not always lead to the place or goal you sought (*You race towards an early grave*).

Wave Riding and Wave Crashing

The image of topping the biggest *wave* is well chosen, as it vividly evokes a person poised within the moment. As opposed to living in the mindful moment from the first verse, however, the life spent moving from exciting moment to exciting moment contemplated in the fourth verse may not sustain you outside of those actual moments. The image is also about being atop the *biggest* wave, though, and from this height you are presumably better able see the choices set out before you. When you select from your choices, you may push yourself into a world that may well push back, and if the moments you choose are in themselves empty once they are experienced, your rush from moment to moment is indeed little more than a rush toward the grave.

The *biggest wave* must be upon an ocean, of course, which evokes the wider world. This suggests that this verse contemplates something much more than the quotidian, day-to-day struggles. It recalls Hamlet's Sea of Troubles, from his famous soliloquy:[68]

---

[68] William Shakespeare, "The Tragedy of Hamlet," in *The Yale Shakespeare: the Complete Works*, ed. Wilbur L. Cross and Tucker Brooke (New York: Barnes & Noble Books, 1993), p. 995

To be, or not to be, that is the question:

Whether 'tis nobler in the mind to suffer

The slings and arrows of outrageous fortune,

Or to take Arms against a Sea of troubles,

And by opposing end them: to die, to sleep

No more; and by a sleep, to say we end

the heart-ache, and the thousand natural shocks

that Flesh is heir to? 'Tis a consummation

devoutly to be wished. To die, to sleep,

To sleep, perchance to Dream; aye, there's the rub,

for in that sleep of death, what dreams may come,

when we have shuffled off this mortal coil,

must give us pause.

Hamlet's struggle is whether or not to oppose the sea of troubles that his life has become. Hamlet appears believe that there is no alternative to the ongoing thoughtlessness, injustice, vulgarity, and cruelty of life except suicide. But in Hamlet's formulation, the choice presupposes that life — The slings and arrows of outrageous fortune — is suffered, that it is something inescapably imposed upon you with the miserable vastness of the sea.

Within the play, it makes perfect sense. *The Tragedy of Hamlet, Prince of Denmark*, is a very complicated sea of troubles, churning and frothing around Hamlet himself.

This sea is manifest from the very start: The play begins with Hamlet coming home to grieve his murdered father, the King of Denmark, and finding the King's brother, Claudius, on the throne. The ghost of his father appears to Hamlet and commands Hamlet to avenge him by killing King Claudius, whom the ghost says murdered him. Hamlet does this, after some famous vacillation. Suffering accumulates through the play, with a mistaken stabbing, suicidal drowning, poisoned wine and poisoned swords, and much pontification about murder and its meaning. A troubled sea indeed.

"Breathe" offers a different point of view on that same sea, however, by proposing that one may lift oneself above misery, and balance on that biggest wave. It suggests that while life can be a struggle against overwhelming conditions, the hero can nonetheless prevail. In this, "Breathe" calls to mind the famous Katsushika Hokusai woodblock print, *Under the Wave off Kanagawa*, more commonly known as *The Great Wave*.

(III, i, 63-75).

14. This 1870 photograph shows the actor Edwin Booth, brother to the today more famous John Wilkes Booth, as Hamlet. The photo, now in the Library of Congress, was taken by J. Gurney & Son, cor. 16th St., N.Y. www.loc.gov/item/2005696075/.

This is one of the most iconic images in the world. It is, of course, striking in composition and execution, and compelling in its subtle comment on the nature of man in his environment. The print is part of a series, *Thirty-six Views of Mount Fuji*. Many casual observers might be surprised by the title of the series and would have to look again to notice that Mount Fuji — the most majestic mountain in all of Japan — is in the painting at all.

The initial impression of the picture is the immense power of the ocean, able to crush anything in its path. This initial impression is important, as it underpins the formidable task the print illustrates. The subject of the print is found in its proper name, *Under the Wave off Kanagawa*. It is the fisherman in their boats contending with the wave, as opposed to the wave itself, that is the subject. Undaunted by this awesome sea, they sally forth. These fishermen, more than Hamlet, seem to capture the spirit of "Breathe."

15. *The Great Wave*, which is the common name for *Under the Wave off Kanagawa (Kanagawa oki nami ura)*, from the series *Thirty-six Views of Mount Fuji (Fugaku sanjūrokkei)* from the Henry L. Phillips Collection, Bequest of Henry L. Phillips, 1939, at the Metropolitan Museum of Art, http://www.metmuseum.org/art/collection/search/56353.

It should be noted that the sea from *Under the Wave off Kanagawa* inspired great music long before *The Dark Side of the Moon*. The cover of the 1905 first edition of the sheet music to Claude Debussy's *La Mer* (*The Sea*) featured a detail from the print.[69] While he was writing the piece, moreover, Debussy had a framed copy of the print itself hanging on his wall.[70]

---

[69] Michael Cirigliano II, "Hokusai and Debussy's Evocations of the Sea," metmuseum.org (The Metropolitan Museum of Art, July 22, 2014), http://www.metmuseum.org/blogs/now-at-the-met/2014/debussy-la-mer.
[70] *Id.*

Just as was Pink Floyd in creating *The Dark Side of the Moon*, Debussy was interested in building a self-contained musical form.[71] Though much of *La Mer* swirls, ebbs and flows, there are occasions (e.g., the middle of the first movement, *De l'aube a midi sur la mer*, especially the final phrases, or approximately a third of the way through the third movement, *Dialogue du vent et de la mer*) where the vast power of the Sea is conveyed in all its orchestral thunder. Such tumult suggests how difficult it would be to live life *balanced on the biggest wave*.

The second and fourth verses of "Breathe" remind us that whether one is rushing toward triumph or disaster cannot always be known beforehand. So much of what comes to us is seemingly cast our way without rhyme or reason, without an apparent pattern that involves a cause-and-effect description. But the choices these circumstances present are constantly set before us to make, which themselves in turn beget new demands for new decisions in light of the consequences of the choice previously made.

That consequences include unintended or unforeseen ramifications is almost always a given. The final verse of "Breathe" insinuates that there may be an escape from the working class or even the white-collar world, by becoming a part of the upper class — *high you fly*. In this way, you may become a part of the controllers of the competitive machinery of business, a part of, rather than pawn of, the tide. Since you are no longer simply a cog in a wheel, it may seem like progress. But that one ramification of this progress is that *You race towards an early grave*, however, reminds you that not all progress is forward.

The idea that a better job or fatter bankbook is not a key to happiness has long been a recurring theme in literature and music. For example, while "Breathe" may not have been directly influenced by Edwin Arlington Robinson's 1897 poem "Richard Cory,"[72] "Breathe" may have resonated with Paul Simon's more recent 1966 version of the poem on the *Sounds of Silence* Simon & Garfunkel album.[73]

In Robinson's version, Richard Cory was a glittering gentleman, richer than a king, while in Simon's version he was a man of power, grace, and style. In both, the presumably impoverished narrator tells how Richard Cory commits suicide one night. Simon's version has the narrator working

[71] Andrew Clements, "Debussy: La Mer," *The Guardian* (Guardian News and Media, March 3, 2000), https://www.theguardian.com/culture/2000/mar/03/classicalmusicandopera.

[72] Edwin Arlington Robinson, "Richard Cory," Poetry Foundation (Poetry Foundation), accessed September 26, 2020, https://www.poetryfoundation.org/poems/44982/richard-cory.

[73] Paul Simon, "Richard Cory," The Paul Simon Official Site, February 1, 2016, https://www.paulsimon.com/song/richard-cory.

in one of Richard Cory's factories, and makes it clear that even so, he wished he were in Richard Cory's place, joining him in death. That the singer is trapped in poverty while working in one of Richard Cory's own factories adds another layer of complexity, however, reminding the listener that there are many paths to misery.

Emerson, Lake and Palmer's "Lucky Man," the single from their self-titled 1970 debut album, has a similar sentiment about the dearth of comfort riches can ultimately bring.[74] Though it may have been the fuzzy Greg Lake guitar, Carl Palmer's military-march snare drum, or Keith Emerson's epic Moog synthesizer solo that initially attracted you, you nonetheless left the song with a lesson. Similar to Richard Cory, the focal character of "Lucky Man" is a rich man, but he is a war hero who is mortally wounded while fighting for his country and his king. Though his riches could not save him, the song nonetheless calls him a lucky man, even as he died.

Neither "Richard Cory" nor "Lucky Man" describes explicitly any hollowness or sadness that either of their protagonists suffers, but the listener understands the lessons there implicitly: Whether it is riches from running a factory or glory on the battlefield, whatever and however much has been won does not in itself stave off despair or death. This begs the question, though, of why one might seek to revel in riches at all. Roger Waters had much the same thoughts as he drafted the vast majority of the lyrics for *The Dark Side of the Moon*, believing that the pursuit of worldly goods obscures the way to a full life.[75]

To listen to "Breathe" is to be reminded that what you seek needs to be what you value; otherwise, what you acquire will not fulfill you or be a comfort to you, but only distract you. When you are caught up in some enterprise you do not intrinsically value, one which does not embody the self you wish to project into your future, you may well be busy and distracted, but you are nonetheless caught up in a race towards an early grave — early, because it ends before it is fulfilled.

As if to underscore the impression of a race toward oblivion, as the song "Breathe" is ending, a racing sound is heard as the next song begins, the instrumental "On The Run."

---

[74] Greg Lake, "Lyrics for Lucky Man by Emerson, Lake & Palmer — Songfacts," Song Meanings at Songfacts (Songfacts, LLC), accessed September 26, 2020, https://www.songfacts.com/lyrics/emerson-lake-palmer/lucky-man.

[75] Kit Rae, "DARK SIDE OF THE MOON BOOTLEG SOUNDCLIPS and Other Stuff."

Track Three: On The Run

"On The Run" begins with a circling, swirling sound accompanied by a quiet but insistent tapping or ticking, little more than the sound of a stopwatch. Beneath this racing clock sound is a growing heavy, throbbing, rhythmic hum that pulses like something from some Industrial, Electronic, or Post-Punk band.

Pink Floyd has always been associated with and recognized as a pioneer in Progressive, Psychedelic, and Space Rock — as the t-shirt says, *Still First in Space*[76] — but they should also be recognized as paving the way for other genres, with their emphasis on synthesizers, looped rhythms, and other effects. Pink Floyd did not avidly pursue these precursors, of course, and were never much interested in bringing clubbers to their feet. They acknowledge this in their 1981 compilation album, which they titled with tongue very much in cheek, *A Collection of Great Dance Songs*.

The swirling sound is soon joined by what sounds like a speeding car from approximately 14 to 30 seconds into the song, falling in tone like the Doppler Effect experienced as a vehicle passes rapidly by. Over the swirling and racing is heard a female announcer announcing departures over a public address system, apparently in an airport or large railway station. The announcement is difficult to understand, but has been reported to be:[77]

> . . . have your hand baggage and passports ready and then follow the green line to customs and then to immigration. BA 255 to Rome, Cairo, Lagos. May I have your attention please. This announcement . . . passengers on BA 255 to Rome, Cairo, Lagos. Will you please . . . at this time . . .

Rome and Cairo can be heard well enough, so we take railway station off the list of possibilities. Of course, an airport is also more in keeping with the *For long you live and high you fly* lyric of "Breathe."

The sound of the speeding car has gone, and the sounds of rushing footsteps begin to take their place, audible by about 40 seconds in. Together, this progression of sounds suggests a narrative of a person rushing to and through the airport — or, as "Breathe" would say, *racing*.

The footsteps as they appear on the album were the work of Alan Parsons, added after the band members had left for the day:[78]

---

[76] Tee shirt logo, widely available.
[77] Kit Rae, "DARK SIDE OF THE MOON BOOTLEG SOUNDCLIPS and Other Stuff."
[78] Bryan Wawzenek, "Pink Floyd's 'The Dark Side of the Moon': A Track-by-Track Guide," Ultimate Classic Rock (Ultimate Classic Rock, Townsquare Media, Inc., March 1, 2018), https://ultimateclassicrock.com/dark-side-of-the-moon-track-by-track.

The footsteps were done by Peter James, the assistant engineer, running around Studio 2, breathing heavily and panting. They loved it when they heard it the next day.

Parsons has said that he took advantage of the band being distracted by televised soccer matches — both Roger Waters and David Gilmour favor Arsenal[79] — and the offbeat BBC comedy *Monty Python's Flying Circus*:[80]

> I was one of a new breed of engineers that didn't mind making criticisms or suggestions that would normally be made by a producer. . . . You could have argued that I should have kept my big mouth shut. And sometimes I did, and sometimes I didn't.

Very appropriately, Parsons was nominated for a Grammy Award for his engineering of *The Dark Side of the Moon*.[81] That said, Parsons has indicated that his role has been unenthusiastically embraced, at best:[82]

> On many occasions I've asked to be recognized for my contributions to *The Dark Side of the Moon*, but both the band and the label have declined to give any sort of gesture towards me.

It is important to emphasize that Parsons himself had inserted these effects, unrequested by and, at least initially, unbeknownst to the band. As will be discussed in the context of "Time," these footsteps are an example of a virtual happenstance, or incident of what may be called synchronicity, becoming a critical element in making the song "On the Run," and the rest of the album, so compelling.

The footsteps fade by about 55 seconds in, but now several new synthesizer sounds swirl around, sounds that could be jets, propeller-driven aircraft, or helicopters passing. As these throb together, another voice is heard: *Live for today, gone tomorrow. That's me. Ha, ha, ha, ha, ha!*[83] Though the public-address voice described above is less than clear, this laugh is unmistakable. Its archetypal character is crystal clear. The laugh is maniacal, what you would expect from the Joker in the regular playing-card deck, or the Fool in the traditional Tarot deck, once again summoning Jung's Trickster.

---

[79] Gaurav Krishnan, "21 Musicians and the Football Clubs They Support," February 11, 2017, https://www.sportskeeda.com/football/21-musicians-football-clubs-they-support/11.

[80] Mark Blake, Comfortably Numb: the inside Story of Pink Floyd (Cambridge, MA: Da Capo Press, Perseus Books Group, 2008), 184.

[81] "Alan Parsons," GRAMMY.com, July 29, 2020, https://www.grammy.com/grammys/artists/alan-parsons/13857.

[82] Rolling Stone, "Alan Parsons on 'Dark Side': 'Roger Knew Something Great Was in the Making'," *Rolling Stone* (Rolling Stone, September 28, 2011), https://www.rollingstone.com/music/news/alan-parsons-on-dark-side-roger-knew-something-great-was-in-the-making-20110928.

[83] Kit Rae, "DARK SIDE OF THE MOON BOOTLEG SOUNDCLIPS and Other Stuff."

16. The Fool from the traditional Tarot deck, as rendered here by Jean Dodal (or Dodali) of Lyon France in the 18th century, is courtesy Bibliothèque nationale de France, département Estampes et photographie, RESERVE BOITE FOL-KH-381 (5, 76).

Beyond the breathless running and the unhinged laughter, the music has a nervous, speeding tempo, driving forward in escalating recklessness. The urgency is compounded further by an ominous moaning sound that is joined at about two minutes twenty-eight seconds by a high-pitched sound like a jet engine noise. By the time another twenty seconds have passed, the engine noise begins to get rougher, as though the plane was in trouble. The laughter returns in much greater mania as the plane founders further and finally crashes and explodes.

By this point, then, the implicit narrative of "On the Run" is of someone speeding to the airport and running to the gate, only for the flight to end in a crash. It seems to end as "Breathe" predicted: *You race towards an early grave.*

But maybe not.

As the sound of the explosion and rending metal is fading, running footsteps are heard, to recede again with the sound of what may be another passing car or far away airplane. It is as though what appeared to be an inescapable, terrible fate had indeed been escaped. This is an idea that will return again much later in the album.

17. On December 9, 2005, Southwest Airlines Flight 1248 crashed into the perimeter fence of Chicago Midway. Photo courtesy National Transportation Safety Board.

Track Four: Time

After the footsteps and vehicle sounds of "On the Run" have gone and the explosion is fading, those sounds are gradually replaced by the ticking of clocks. Many, many clocks. Many different kinds of clocks.

Then they all begin to toll.

And chime.

And ring.

And clang.

So many years later, it may be difficult to remember that first time you heard it, but it seemed every time you played the record you were startled by this return to cacophony. It is as though you had forgotten the lesson of the shrieks in "Speak to Me."

The alarms and clocks go on for nearly half a minute. This is how "Time" begins.

Ticking away the moments that make up a dull day

Fritter and waste the hours in an offhand way.

Kicking around on a piece of ground in your home town

Waiting for someone or something to show you the way.

Tired of lying in the sunshine staying home to watch the rain.

You are young and life is long and there is time to kill today.

And then one day you find ten years have got behind you.

No one told you when to run, you missed the starting gun.

So you run and you run to catch up with the sun but it's sinking

Racing around to come up behind you again.

The sun is the same in a relative way but you're older,

Shorter of breath and one day closer to death.

Every year is getting shorter never seem to find the time.

Plans that either come to naught or half a page of scribbled lines

Hanging on in quiet desperation is the English way

The time is gone, the song is over,

Thought I'd something more to say.

That "Time" begins with this tumult of chiming and clanging clocks was another example of serendipity, or — as discussed below — synchronicity. Alan Parsons had been experimenting on his own with quadraphonic recording of clocks in an antique shop. According to an interview with David Gilmour, Parsons had been unaware of the song "Time" being composed:[84]

> He [Alan Parsons] had just recently before we did that album gone out with a whole set of equipment and had recorded all these clocks in a clock shop. And we were doing the song "Time," and he said "Listen, I just did all these things, I did all these clocks," and so we wheeled out his tape and listened to it and said "Great! Stick it on!" And that, actually, is Alan Parsons' idea.

---

[84] Chris Bell, "a list obligatory. songs about time, vol. 4: the final countdown." Earbuddy (Earbuddy, September 10, 2012), https://www.earbuddy.net/7546/a-list-obligatory-songs-about-time-vol-4-the-final-countdown.html/columns.

Along with the footsteps in "On the Run," interesting coincidences within the final form of *The Dark Side of the Moon* as released are accumulating. These uncanny coincidences call to mind another of Carl Jung's important ideas, that of Synchronicity. Synchronicity was a word coined by Jung to describe those surprising coincidences or startling collocations and combinations that occur that have no discernible scientific explanation, where cause and effect seem to be absent.

Jung had studied phenomena that appear to contain an element of chance, and yet appear to produce something more — like the *I Ching*, the ancient Chinese method of divining the future from the patterns that result from casting and interpreting a number of symbolic lots.[85] Jung had extensive correspondence with the physicist Wolfgang Pauli prior to writing his book, *Synchronicity: An Acausal Connecting Principle*.[86] Wolfgang Pauli, who won the 1945 Nobel Prize in Physics, helped establish the quantum theory of fields using the statistical behavior of elementary particles.[87]

Jung even discussed his ideas with Albert Einstein, whom he had had as a dinner guest several times when Einstein was a professor in Zurich, and still developing his Theory of Relativity.[88] Albert Einstein, of course, is the physicist responsible for the development of the Theory of Relativity, which postulates that time and space are not two different things at all, nor are matter and energy, and that what we think of as results of the force of gravity are governed by the bending of space-time by matter.

Through his studies, and his dialogues with Einstein and Pauli, Jung theorized that ordinary thinking with respect to time and space was insufficient to explain meaningful coincidences:[89]

> Synchronicity is not a philosophical view but an empirical concept which postulates an intellectually necessary principle. This cannot be called either materialism or metaphysics. No serious investigator would assert that the nature of what is observed to exist, and of that which observes, namely the psyche, are known and recognized quantities. If the latest conclusions of science are coming nearer and nearer to a unitary idea of being, characterized by space and time on the one hand and by causality and synchronicity on the other, that has nothing to do with materialism. Rather it seems to show that there is

---

[85] The Editors of Encyclopaedia Britannica, "Yijing ancient Chinese text," *Encyclopædia Britannica* (Encyclopædia Britannica, Inc., November 2, 2017), https://www.britannica.com/topic/Yijing.

[86] Carl Gustav Jung, *Synchronicity: An Acausal Connecting Principle*, ed. Michael Fordham, trans. Richard Francis Carrington. Hull, 2nd ed. (Princeton: Princeton University Press, 1973).

[87] *Nobel Lectures: Physics: 1942–1962* (Amsterdam: Published for the Nobel Foundation by Elsevier, 1964).

[88] *Id.*, Michael Fordam, Editorial Preface, p. vi.

[89] Carl Jung, *Synchronicity*, p. 96.

some possibility of getting rid of the incommensurability between the observed and the observer. The result, in that case, would be a unity of being which would have to be expressed in terms of a new conceptual language — a "neutral language," as W. Pauli once called it.

Space, time, and causality, the triad of classical physics, would then be supplemented by the synchronicity factor . . .

The development of this concept was deeply rooted in Jung's own personal perception of reality:[90]

. . . I never entirely freed myself of the impression that this life is a segment of existence which is enacted in a three-dimensional boxlike universe especially set up for it.

Though the idea of synchronicity may seem far-fetched, it should be remembered that Einstein himself had long maintained that time was an illusion. When his close friend Michele Besso died, Einstein wrote to Besso's family:[91]

Now he has departed this strange world a little ahead of me. That signifies nothing. For us believing physicists, the distinction between past, present and future is only a stubbornly persistent illusion.

Besso and Einstein had been students together and then worked together in the federal patent office in Berne, Switzerland.[92] Besso was given a special acknowledgment in Einstein's original, groundbreaking paper on Special Relativity, the only person to have been so memorialized:[93]

In conclusion I wish to say that in working at the problem here dealt with I have had the loyal assistance of my friend and colleague M. Besso, and that I am indebted to him for several valuable suggestions.

When the eminent physicist Stephen Hawking edited Einstein's collected works, he actually named the collection *A Stubbornly Persistent Illusion: The Essential Scientific Works of Albert Einstein*. In Hawking's Introduction, he provides a quote which may shed light on Einstein's discussions with Jung:[94]

---

[90] Carl Jung, *Memories, Dreams, Reflections*, p. 295.

[91] Dan Falk and Quanta, "The Debate Over Time's Place in the Universe," *The Atlantic* (Atlantic Media Company, July 26, 2016), https://www.theatlantic.com/science/archive/2016/07/the-debate-over-times-place-in-the-universe/492464.

[92] Thomas Venning, "Time's Arrow: Albert Einstein's Letters to Michele Besso: Christie's," Einstein's letters to Michele Besso | Christie's (Christies, November 14, 2017), https://www.christies.com/features/Einstein-letters-to-Michele-Besso-8422-1.aspx.

[93] H. A. Lorentz et al., "The Principle of Relativity. Memoirs on the Special and General Theory of Relativity," ed. A. Sommerfeld, trans. W. Perrett and G. B. Jeffery, Internet Archive (Dover, October 11, 2013), https://archive.org/details/principlerelativ00halo/page/n69/mode/2up, p. 65.

[94] Steven Hawking, Introduction, Albert Einstein and Stephen Hawking, *A Stubbornly Persistent Illusion the Essential Scientific Writings of Albert Einstein* (Philadelphia: Running Press, 2009), p. xi.

"At a time like the present," Einstein wrote, "when experience forces us to seek a newer and more solid foundation, the physicist cannot simply surrender to the philosopher the critical contemplation of the theoretical foundations; for, he himself knows best, and feels more surely where the shoe pinches."

18. This photograph of Einstein and his wife, taken approximately 1915, is courtesy Library of Congress, George Grantham Bain Collection. https://www.loc.gov/item/2014712249/.

That is, it does not appear that Einstein, the physicist, would leave Jung, in this case a philosopher rather than psychologist, to determine how the world works on his own. Synchronicity might thus be an explanation for another instance of remarkable coincidence reflected in "Time."

Illusions of Time and Consciousness

That Einstein calls the difference between past, present, and future an illusion is for him a gateway to understanding the physics of space-time. The complement to Einstein's physical idea is to look at the psychological basis of understanding time. This would hinge, presumably, on how things such as the passage of time are understood at all. In Julian Jaynes' 1976 book *The Origin of Consciousness in The Breakdown of the Bicameral Mind* — which despite its daunting title was a best-seller —, the American researcher and teacher of psychology at Yale and Princeton challenged the idea that consciousness — where understanding and illusion reside — is itself a continuum:[95]

> The timing of consciousness is also an interesting question. When we are awake, are we conscious all the time? We think so. In fact, we are sure so! I shut my eyes and even if I try not to think, consciousness still streams on, a great river of contents in a succession of different conditions which I have been taught to call thoughts, images, memories, interior dialogues, regrets, wishes, resolves, all interweaving with the constantly changing pageant of exterior sensations of which I am selectively aware. Always the continuity. Certainly this is the feeling. And what-ever we're doing, we feel that our very self, our deepest of deep identity, is indeed this continuing flow that only ceases in sleep between remembered dreams. This is our experience. And many thinkers have taken this spirit of continuity to be the place to start from in philosophy, the very ground of certainty which no one can doubt. Cogito, ergo sum.
>
> But what could this continuity mean? If we think of a minute as being sixty thousand milliseconds, are we conscious for every one of those milliseconds? If you still think so, go on dividing the time units, remembering that the firing of neurons is of a finite order — although we have no idea what that has to do with our sense of the continuity of consciousness. Few persons would wish to maintain that consciousness somehow floats like a mist above and about the nervous system completely ununited to any earthly necessities of neural refractory periods.
>
> It is much more probable that the seeming continuity of consciousness is really an illusion, just as most of the other metaphors about consciousness are.

Jean-Paul Sartre, for whom consciousness is always consciousness *of* something,[96] viewed time in a way that seems like one which both Einstein and Jaynes would approve:[97]

> If Time is considered by itself, it immediately dissolves into an absolute multiplicity of instants which considered separately lose all temporal nature and are reduced purely and simply to the total atemporality of the *this*. . . . In fact our first apprehension of objective time is *practical*: it is while *being* my possibilities beyond co-present being that I discover objective time as the worldly correlate of nothingness which separates me from my possible. . . .

---

[95] *Julian Jaynes, The Origin of Consciousness in the Breakdown of the Bicameral Mind* (Boston: Houghton Mifflin, 1976), pp. 23-24.

[96] Hazel E. Barnes, Translator's Introduction, Jean-Paul Sartre, *Being and Nothingness: an Essay on Phenomenological Ontology*, Barnes, tr. and introd Hazel E. Barnes (New York: Philosophical Library 1966), p. xii.

[97] *Id.*, Part Two, Chapter Three, Section IV, p. 294 (italics original).

. . . Then the *lapse* of time disappears, and time is revealed as the shimmer of nothingness on the surface of a strictly atemporal being.

As Alan Parson's clanging and chiming, ringing and booming finally fade, another ticking has taken over, a distinctive tom-tom sound produced by a drum called a Rototom. Synchronicity is potentially found in that the drummer Nick Mason said that the Rototoms had just been left in the studio by whoever had happened to use the space before them. He had never seen Rototoms before and just started tinkering with them, ultimately using them in "Time."[98] It is difficult now to imagine "Time" without that sound.

The Rototom is soon joined by slow, heavy bass notes, by sounds resembling bell-like xylophone or vibraphone notes, and then by guitar and synthesizer. A generally upbeat instrumental continues for about two and a half minutes. This instrumental is brought up sharply, however, with abrupt raps on drums and the rapid, insistent, almost shrill vocals of the first verse:

Ticking away the moments that make up a dull day

You fritter and waste the hours in an offhand way.

Kicking around on a piece of ground in your home town

Waiting for someone or something to show you the way.

The phrase *fritter and waste the hours*, combined with the overall gloomy outlook of "Time," seems to resonate with the "struts and frets his hour" soliloquy of Shakespeare's *Macbeth*:[99]

To-morrow, and to-morrow, and to-morrow,

Creeps in this petty pace from day to day

To the last syllable of recorded time,

And all our yesterdays have lighted fools

The way to dusty death. Out, out, brief candle!

Life's but a walking shadow, a poor player

That struts and frets his hour upon the stage

And then is heard no more: it is a tale

Told by an idiot, full of sound and fury,

Signifying nothing.

[98] Tom Schäfer, "Nick Mason: Der Rhythmusarchitekt Von Pink Floyd," *STICKS* (EBNER MEDIA GROUP GMBH & CO. KG, January 27, 2016), https://www.sticks.de/stories/nick-mason-der-rhythmusarchitekt-von-pink-floyd.

[99] William Shakespeare, "The Tragedy of Macbeth," in *The Yale Shakespeare*, p. 1149 (V, v, 20-29).

Macbeth, it appears from this famous quotation, obviously lamented the way our lives are frittered pointlessly away day by day. He would empathize with the notion of racing toward an early grave or the vanity of digging hole after hole in "Breathe," though he might well maintain that the holes that are being dug are all graves.

Shakespeare's play, *The Tragedy of Macbeth*, casts a shadow over Macbeth himself, who is steeped in the prophecies of three witches. Macbeth has killed his king, Duncan, usurped Duncan's throne, and had assassins kill Banquo, a former friend whom Macbeth believes will expose the murder. Macbeth then commits more murders after Banquo's ghost appears to him.

Macbeth then seeks — and misunderstands — further prophecies from the witches, which turn out to be more cryptic than they might have first appeared. Ultimately the prophecies are fulfilled, and Macbeth is beheaded by Macduff, whose family Macbeth had killed. The throne of Scotland is finally filled by Malcolm, son of the earlier-murdered Duncan.

19. This painting of William Shakespeare, originally copyrighted by Eugene A. Perry in 1907, is The Perry Pictures, no. 73, Boston edition, courtesy Library of Congress. https://www.loc.gov/item/2003653783/.

Such a morose outlook is in keeping with the slowing tempo of the second verse of "Time," and the quavering female voices surrounding the lead vocal in lush ooo-ing could well be the three witches from Macbeth. This tormented choir intensifies the gloom of the next verse in "Time" with an undercurrent of mystery and vague foreboding:

Tired of lying in the sunshine staying home to watch the rain.

You are young and life is long and there is time to kill today.

And then one day you find ten years have got behind you.

No one told you when to run, you missed the starting gun.

With the phrase *starting gun*, the tempo of *Time* speeds up again, breaking into a cavernous, classic stadium rock guitar solo. Toward the end of the solo, the bewitched choir begins again, ebbing and flowing easily for a few moments before rising briefly almost into a shout as the third verse begins:

So you run and you run to up with the sun but it's sinking

Racing around to come up behind you again.

The sun is the same in a relative way but you're older,

Shorter of breath and one day closer to death.

The choir of women's voices joins up again to surround the fourth verse, this time sounding more mournful than menacing:

Every year is getting shorter never seem to find the time.

Plans that either come to naught or half a page of scribbled lines

Hanging on in quiet desperation is the English way

The time is gone, the song is over,

Thought I'd something more to say.

The Deep Roots of Quiet Desperation

This sense of fruitless pursuit is not an idea sprung from the Industrial Revolution or Shakespeare, but has been well known for thousands of years, since at least the time of the Old Testament. The Book of Ecclesiastes begins:[100]

Vanity of vanities, says the Preacher,

vanity of vanities! All is vanity.

What does man gain by all the toil

at which he toils under the sun?

---

[100] Eccl 1-6, "Bible Gateway Passage: Ecclesiastes 1 — English Standard Version," Bible Gateway (Good News Publishers), accessed October 4, 2020, https://www.bible-gateway.com/passage/?search=Ecclesiastes+1&version=ESV.

A generation goes, and a generation comes,

> but the earth remains forever.

The sun rises, and the sun goes down,

> and hastens to the place where it rises.

The wind blows to the south

> and goes around to the north;

around and around goes the wind,

> and on its circuits the wind returns.

This passage seems an obvious possible inspiration for parts of "Breathe" and "Time." The idea is made even more interesting by reference to alternative translations of the original Hebrew for vanity. For example, footnotes to the above passage, taken from Bible Gateway, indicate that in this verse, Ecclesiastes 1:2:[101]

> The Hebrew term *hebel*, translated *vanity* or *vain*, refers concretely to a "mist," "vapor," or "mere breath," and metaphorically to something that is fleeting or elusive (with different nuances depending on the context).

Note also how similar this analysis is to that discussed in the "Speak to Me" chapter, in which Jung analyzed his patient's dream of her father rocking her in his arms as the wheat swayed in the wind. Hence, while "mere breath" may be valued in mindful focus, as emphasized in "Breathe," "Time" rejects the idea that one may find solace in any undertaking of any kind without sincere commitment. And so it is without solace that the vast majority of people pass their time, hanging on in their quiet desperation.

Of course, quiet desperation is not limited to the English: As succinctly stated by Henry David Thoreau in *Walden, or Life in the Woods*, "The mass of men lead lives of quiet desperation." [102] Thoreau goes on in the very next paragraph to sourly observe:[103]

> Age is no better, hardly so well, qualified for an instructor as youth, for it has not profited so much as it has lost. One may almost doubt if the wisest man has learned anything of absolute value by living. Practically, the old have no very important advice to give the young, their own experience has been so partial, and their lives have been such miserable failures, for private reasons, as they must believe; and it may

---

[101] *Id.* at footnote b.

[102] Henry David Thoreau, *Walden; or, Life in the Woods, and On the Duty of Civil Disobedience* (New York: Signet, 1963), page 10. Available online at "Walden; or, Life in the Woods," Internet Archive (Boston Public Library (Rare Books Department), Ticknor and Fields, January 1, 1970), https://archive.org/details/waldenorlifeinwo1854thor.

[103] *Id.* at page 11.

be that they have some faith left which belies that experience, and they are only less young than they were.

Elsewhere in *Walden*, as though commenting on the line in "Time," *Thought I'd something more to say*, Thoreau observes, "The commonest sense is the sense of men asleep, which they express by snoring."[104]

There is no snoring in "Time." As indicated above, harmonizing female voices intermittently accompany the lead singer in "Time," starting with the phrase, *Tired of lying in the sunshine*. They sing together for most of the song, perhaps representing the population at large, as was the case since at least the ancient Greeks. A Greek chorus did not usually move the song or action forward as such, but instead commented on the actions of the heroes and heroines, reflecting the popular hopes and fears.[105]

20. This photograph of Henry David Thoreau, head-and-shoulders portrait, facing slightly right, ca. 1879, courtesy Library of Congress. https://www.loc.gov/item/95513963/.

[104] *Id.* at page 347.
[105] Adam Augustyn, "Chorus," *Encyclopædia Britannica* (Encyclopædia Britannica, Inc.), accessed November 23, 2020, https://www.britannica.com/art/chorus-theatre.

In this case, their choral unity in "Time" may reflect the way most typical and routine experiences slip by almost without notice. These fleeting phenomena nonetheless accumulate day upon day — like snowflakes, each a small thing on its own, easily ignored, but piling up until they have become a snow drift against which you cannot open your door.

Toward the end of "Time," however, one voice separates itself out, beginning with the phrase, *Never seem to find the time*, about 5 minutes and 18 seconds into the song. While it foreshadows the powerful female solo on "The Great Gig In The Sky," which is described below in its own chapter, the solo in "Time" is relatively brief and, as opposed to the vast spectrum explored by "The Great Gig In The Sky," does not display a very broad range of emotions. Instead, it is a few moments of wordless lament.

The song ends with the other female voices joined again, as if in sympathy with the one keening, or to signal their collective resignation to their lost, misspent time. Such disconsolate feelings reflect an epiphany for Roger Waters that caught him up as Pink Floyd worked on the album. Waters realized that there was no bright-line delineation between your youth and adulthood, no separation of getting ready for and then living your life. "Time" and "Breathe" reflect these revelations, that the here and now are what make up your life.[106]

Though there may not be a clear distinction between preparation and life, the lyrics in "Time" nonetheless reflect well the conflicting forces the young adult faces with the abrupt disappearance of guidance and supervision. For so many years of childhood, adolescence, and early adult life, most of their life has been framed with other people's expectations, being told in one way or another what to do.

Those expectations have been predominantly societal in nature — that is, for the general community at-large, and not developed with one individual's specific, personal propensities and abilities in mind. Thus, while the hours in a day may be allocated in a certain ways to keep juveniles busy or at least out from underfoot — "breakfast," "school," "play" for the children; "work," "homework," and "rest" for the slightly older. Though this carries the majority through to adulthood, there will always be individuals not entirely engaged by activities, individuals who realize the parade is ultimately directionless:

> Ticking away the moments that make up a dull day
>
> You fritter and waste the hours in an offhand way.
>
> Kicking around on a piece of ground in your home town,

[106] MOJO Staff, "MOJO Issue 193 / December 2009," *Mojo* (Bauer Media Group, December 17, 2009), https://www.mojo4music.com/articles/2420/mojo-issue-193-december-2009.

Waiting for someone or something to show you the way.

This verse, especially the word *ground*, reminds you of the first verse of "Breathe," where you were exhorted to *choose your own ground* rather than to simply acquiesce to what you were given. That is, in "Breathe," you are essentially exhorted to get up and leave. In "Time," in contrast, you are hanging out *on a piece of ground in your home town* basically because it was where you were when you were born. This verse in "Time" is a caution of the consequences of not heeding the call to action in "Breathe."

All people are born into a set of circumstances that was not of their choosing in any feature or detail. Professor Jacques Salvan examined Jean-Paul Sartre's major philosophical work *Being and Nothingness* in his own book, *To Be and Not To Be: An Analysis of Jean-Paul Sartre's Ontology.* In the Introduction to his book, Salvan captures the sense in which our lives begin with conditions over which we had no choice, which seemingly arose by chance:[107]

> If, for a moment, as I reflect upon the fact of my existence, I refrain from considering myself as a man among other men, participating of the abstract character of mortal Man and sharing the essence of mortal Man, if I turn my attention to the actuality of my existence and come to wonder why I exist as a man, why I was born, let us say, at the turn of the century in a family of up-state New York Republicans belonging to the Episcopalian Church, why I am meditating here and now upon that fact, I can hardly fail to realize, probably with some sort of awe and wonder, that the question cannot be answered, that I just happen to have been born in such circumstances, that, in other words, my existence is entirely contingent.

Because one has not chosen one's background, each person must decide either to choose your own ground, or to instead fester, as described in "Time," soaked in ennui, *lying in the sunshine staying home to watch the rain.* This latter line strongly resonates with The Beatles' 1967 song from their Magical Mystery Tour album, "I Am The Walrus:"[108]

> *Sitting in an English garden, waiting for the sun.*
>
> *If the sun don't come you get a tan*
>
> *From standing in the English rain.*

This resonance suggests that the English are inured to the rain completely. It's not so bad, you may think; it passes the time until something comes along

---

[107] Jacques Léon Salvan, *To Be and Not to Be. An Analysis of Jean-Paul Sartre's Ontology*, ed. Ita Kanter (Detroit, MI: Wayne State University Press, 1962), p. xi.

[108] John Lennon and Paul McCartney, "I Am the Walrus (Lennon-McCartney)," Beatles Lyrics: I am the Walrus (BeatlesLyrics.org), accessed October 9, 2020, https://www.beatleslyrics.org/index_files/Page7413.htm.

to take you to the next stage of your life: *You are young and life is long and there is time to kill today*.

21. French journalists visiting General George C. Marshall in the Pentagon. Left to right: seated, General Marshall, Mme Etiennette Benichon, Louis Lombard; standing, François Prieur, Jean-Paul Sartre, Stephane Pizella, and Pierre Denoyer. Washington, D.C, March 1945. Photograph by Lakey Sherrel courtesy Library of Congress. https://www.loc.gov/item/2017869622/.

That you have time to waste is not a new outlook, and a familiar feeling to many people. Many others, however, seem to require someone else to draw attention to its potential peril. Robert Herrick, for example, made the point centuries before, in the year 1648, of opportunities fruitlessly passing, when he published "To the Virgins, to Make Much of Time," which starts right off with a caution about the ephemeral nature of beauty:[109]

GATHER ye rosebuds while ye may,

Old Time is still a-flying:

And this same flower that smiles to-day

To-morrow will be dying.

[109] Robert Herrick, "To the Virgins, to Make Much of Time," in Eleanor Fortescue-Brickdale, ed., "The Book of Old English Songs and Ballads," Internet Archive (Hodder and Stoughton, University of California Libraries, December 14, 2007), https://archive.org/details/bookofoldenglish00fortrich, p.192.

Herrick's "To the Virgins" might have been the very poem on Roger Waters' mind as he wrote the next few lines of "Time:"

So you run and you run to catch up with the sun but it's sinking

Racing around to come up behind you again.

The sun is the same in a relative way but you're older,

Shorter of breath and one day closer to death.

Compare this measuring of your life against the practically infinite life of the sun to the second stanza of "To the Virgins:" [110]

The glorious lamp of heaven, the sun,

The higher he's a-getting,

The sooner will his race be run,

And nearer he's to setting.

In the balance of the poem, though, Herrick is more gentle and positive in his warning about just letting time pass:[111]

That age is best which is the first,

When youth and blood are warmer;

But being spent, the worse, and worst

Times still succeed the former.

Then be not coy, but use your time,

And while ye may, go marry:

For having lost but once your prime,

You may for ever tarry.

Other views, however, are not so gentle. Saul Bellow, for example, who won the 1976 Nobel Prize in Literature,[112] deftly captured the burden of knowing that one has actually chosen to waste away one's time. Think of the main character, Joseph, in Saul Bellow's 1944 novella, *Dangling Man*, who initially drifts aimlessly through things, thinking that his draft notice will come up soon. In 1972, as *The Dark Side of the Moon* was evolving, draft notices for the Vietnam War were very much on many people's minds, and this approach to life would have had great resonance.

---

[110] *Id.*

[111] *Id.*

[112] "The Nobel Prize in Literature 1976," NobelPrize.org (Nobel Media AB), accessed December 28, 2020, https://www.nobelprize.org/prizes/literature/1976/summary.

As the days of waiting grow into months, however, Bellow's *Dangling Man* thinks about and then rejects going back to work while he waits. As he waits, though, his idleness becomes heavy:[113]

> There is nothing to do but wait, or dangle, and grow more and more dispirited. It is perfectly clear to me that I am deteriorating, storing bitterness and spite which eat like acids at my endowment of generosity and good will.

Hence, though Bellow's *Dangling Man* recognizes the waste of his time and its corrosive effect on him, he nonetheless resigns himself — that is, makes a decision — to "wait, or dangle, and grow more and more dispirited." Similarly, it is the explicit realization that his time is being frittered away that distinguishes the speaker in "Time" from one who is unaware or is inured to the passing of misspent time. Instead, the speaker in "Time" brings himself up short at the thought that his life is going on without himself at the wheel:

> *And then one day you find ten years have got behind you.*
>
> *No one told you when to run, you missed the starting gun.*

In this verse, at least initially, the speaker in "Time" does not get mired in regret or inertia, but affirmatively takes the wheel of his life and seeks to catch up with what should have been (*So you run and you run to catch up with the sun*). That *Carpe Diem* spirit, however, seems to bleed away by the sustained effort it requires:

> *Every year is getting shorter never seem to find the time.*
>
> *Plans that either come to naught or half a page of scribbled lines*

The realization that one must affirmatively take control of one's life is eroded by the myriad distractions one allows between the intention to do something and actually doing it. The failure to make your own life a priority accumulates, and within the span you are given, your life becomes a cascade of half-measures.

We have seen this before. Think, for example, of T.S. Eliot's 1920 poem, "The Love Song of J. Alfred Prufrock," whose deep contemplations of his life are often indistinguishable from woolgathering:[114]

> For I have known them all already, known them all:
>
> Have known the evenings, mornings, afternoons,
>
> I have measured out my life with coffee spoons;

---

[113] Saul Bellow, *Dangling Man* (New York: Signet, 1974), p. 12. Available online at "Dangling Man," Internet Archive (Digital Library of India, September 22, 2015), https://archive.org/details/in.ernet.dli.2015.470139.

[114] T. S. Eliot, "Prufrock and Other Observations," Internet Archive (The Egoist Ltd., University of California Libraries, November 17, 2006), https://archive.org/details/prufrockandother00eliorich, p. 39.

I know the voices dying with a dying fall

Beneath the music from a farther room.

So how should I presume?

22. Cover of the 1882 edition *Selections from the poetry of Robert Herrick*, illustrated by Edwin Austin Abbey, courtesy of Library of Congress. https://www.loc.gov/item/2010714810/.

23. T. S. Eliot was the winner of the 1948 Nobel Prize for Literature. Photograph courtesy Archivo Historico Sinaloa.

Though Eliot wrote profoundly modern poetry that was nonetheless deeply rooted in ancient literature and philosophy, no one better captured the weight of indecision than Eliot. How similar to Eliot's bleak resignation is the sense of futility and timidity in "Time:"

Hanging on in quiet desperation is the English way

The time is gone, the song is over,

Thought I'd something more to say.

And so in both "Breathe" and in "Time" there is the explicit recognition of personal responsibility for all the choices you make, but also illustration of the burdens, trade-offs, and double edges associated with the choices. The responsibility is inescapable, as the philosopher Jean-Paul Sartre has said in his major work, *Being and Nothingness:*[115]

---

[115] Jean-Paul Sartre, *Being and Nothingness*, p. 567.

I am condemned to be free. This means that no limits to my freedom can be found except freedom itself or, if you prefer, that we are not free to cease being free.

The idea that freedom cannot be evaded or excused away seems a key formulation, insofar as Sartre phrases it in very much the same way in *Existentialism and Humanism*:[116]

Man is condemned to be free; because once thrown into the world, he is responsible for everything he does. It is up to you to give [life] a meaning.

The speaker in "Time" is not intellectually obsessed with the waste of so much of life, as Sartre often seemed to be, but the regrets are clear. As in "Breathe," the speaker in "Time" is aware that he can and should make more of himself and his life, but the making of choices and readjusting to consequences are daily demands that the speaker does not seem up to. For the speakers in "Time" and "Breathe," their struggle against complacency and inertia just does not engage their full attention.

No single day's failure is of cataclysmic importance, perhaps, but the accumulated loss of those days nonetheless can weigh on the mind and heart of the speaker. And yet that life can end at any time, taking with it the opportunity to choose anything different in that life. Like Kierkegaard had observed above regarding the final closure brought by death, the character Inès states in Sartre's play *No Exit*:[117]

One always dies too soon — or too late. And yet, one's whole life is complete at that moment, with a line drawn neatly under it, ready for the summing up. You are — your life, and nothing else.

No Exit was perhaps Sartre's most successful play, which is compelling despite its formal simplicity. In *No Exit*, three strangers find themselves locked in a room after their deaths. It is a decidedly awkward threesome in this single room: Garcin appears to be in hell because he'd been unfaithful and abusive to his wife. Estelle had an affair with a younger man after marrying an old man for his money. The affair resulted in a child, whom Estelle drowned, driving her young lover to commit suicide. Inès seduced her cousin's wife and turned her against her husband, ultimately leading to the murder of the cousin. Thus, while it is apparently just a plain room, the idea that they are locked together for eternity makes it hell to each of them.

The play examines how in life people may deceive themselves and rely on the judgment of others to take the place of their own responsibility for

---

[116] Jean-Paul Sartre, *Existentialism and Humanism*, p. 34.

[117] Jean-Paul Sartre, "No Exit," in *No Exit and Three Other Plays* (New York: Vintage Books, 1955), p. 45. Available online at Internet Archive, October 7, 2011, https://archive.org/details/NoExit.

the choices they have made. As each seeks approval or forgiveness from the others, *No Exit* explores themes of cowardice, lust, and cruelty, and contains in its last moments Garcin's famous line, "Hell is — other people!"[118] Thus, when one has abrogated his or her responsibility for their choices, one becomes endlessly at the mercy of others' standards. Another's unsympathetic conceptions of one's self-worth and identity could indeed be a hell.

This ongoing tension between what is and what could have been, and the inexorable personal responsibility for however large the difference between the two, is dramatically reflected by the music in "Time." It moves from the ticking of clocks in an antique shop, to a blistering, stadium-filling guitar solo, becoming one of the more rocking songs Pink Floyd has produced, but then falling again to hushed, furtive, church-choir voices.

"Time" seamlessly becomes the contemplative "Breathe Reprise," which sheds new light on the previous songs.

Track Five: Breathe Reprise

"Breathe Reprise" may or may not be designated as a separate song on *The Dark Side of the Moon*, depending on where you look. On the song listing at the top left side of the inner gatefold of the album cover, there are five songs on Side One, five songs on Side Two. "Breathe (Reprise)" is not spelled out as one of the Side One songs there. It is also missing from the labels on the record. In the lyrics printed across the gatefold below the heartbeat, however, it is given a separate heading after "Time." Even there, however, it is distinguished from the other songs, all of whose titles are in all capital letters; "Breathe Reprise" is initial caps only.

While these features might suggest that "Breathe Reprise" is somehow of less importance than the other songs, it is in fact a key pivot-point for the album, expanding on the ideas already shared and introducing new concepts critical to *The Dark Side of the Moon* as a whole.

While it follows the melody of "Breathe," "Breathe Reprise" is slower, more solemn. Like "Breathe," its verse as written inside the gatefold is eight lines long:

> *Home, home again.*
>
> *I like to be here when I can.*
>
> *When I come home cold and tired*
>
> *It's good to warm my bones beside the fire.*
>
> *Far away across the field*

---

[118] *Id.*, p. 47.

> *The tolling of the iron bell*
>
> *Calls the faithful to their knees*
>
> *To hear the softly spoken magic spells.*

As was also the case with "Breathe," however, "Breathe Reprise" seems better read as four-line stanzas.

The first stanza could well be, figuratively, the evening song of the hole-digging rabbit from "Breathe," gone to work before the sun has risen and only coming home after it has set. He has not looked around and chosen his own ground, but has instead sheltered for the night in a familiar room, going through rituals as ancient as man plowing fields or digging mines.

There is no existential angst here; instead, it is a moment of peace after a hard day's work.

> *Home, home again.*
>
> *I like to be here when I can.*
>
> *When I come home cold and tired*
>
> *It's good to warm my bones beside the fire.*

This moment of calm comes only a few minutes after "Time" has reproached the idea of home as a capitulation: *Kicking around on a piece of ground in your home town.* In contrast to "Time," however, where the protagonist is essentially just loitering aimlessly at home, being home in "Breathe Reprise" is clearly the result of a choice to be there: *I like to be here when I can.*

We do not know what work it is that the hero here is sitting down from, but we can infer that it is hard, outdoor work from his coming home cold and tired, and his contentment to sit beside a warm fire. Whatever his work, though, he has come to terms with it. In this sense, it brings to mind the famously counter-intuitive satisfaction of Sisyphus as described in Albert Camus' titular essay in *The Myth of Sisyphus and Other Essays*. In that essay, as in the myth itself, Sisyphus is yoked to the most absurd of labors for having tricked the gods:[119]

> The gods had condemned Sisyphus to ceaselessly rolling a rock to the top of a mountain, whence the stone would fall back of its own weight. They had thought with some reason that there is no more dreadful punishment than futile and hopeless labor.

Camus describes how he imagines Sisyphus' labor vividly:[120]

> As for this myth, one sees merely the whole effort of a body straining to raise the huge stone, to roll it and push it up a slope a hundred times over; one sees the face screwed up, the cheek tight against the stone,

---

[119] Albert Camus, *The Myth of Sisyphus and Other Essays*, p. 88.

[120] *Id.* at p. 89.

the shoulder bracing the clay-covered mass, the foot wedging it, the fresh start with arms outstretched, the wholly human security of two earth-clotted hands. At the very end of his long effort measured by skyless space and time without depth, the purpose is achieved. Then Sisyphus watches the stone rushes down in a few moments toward that lower world whence he will have to push it up again toward the summit.

Notwithstanding this absurdity, however, Camus imagines Sisyphus to be happy in his circumstances. Camus asserts that Sisyphus' happiness lies in rejecting the gods' desire that he cling to the hope that one day the rock will not fall, instead fully embracing his task as wholly his own:[121]

> All Sisyphus' silent joy is contained therein. His fate belongs to him. His rock is his thing. Likewise, the absurd man, when he contemplates his torment, silences all the idols. In the universe suddenly restored to its silence, the myriad wondering little voices of the earth rise up. Unconscious, secret calls, invitations from all the faces, they are the necessary reverse and price of victory. There is no sun without shadow, and it is essential to know the night. The absurd man says yes and his effort will henceforth be unceasing. If there is a personal fate, there is no higher destiny, or at least there is — but one which he concludes is inevitable and despicable. For the rest, he knows himself to be the master of his days.

It is not that the rolling of his stone becomes anything other than what it has always been, but it is that Sisyphus has renounced his desire that it was something else. In renouncing his desire that his existence be other than it is, he has triumphed over the despair inherent in such desires. He chooses how he feels about his life, and thus becomes its master. In this way, Sisyphus can embrace the absurd without the anxiety or angst often associated with such an existentially grounded recognition of the absurd.

In his rejection of the gods' view that his existence must be punishment, Sisyphus can be seen as happier with his present than it seems the characters in *No Exit* are able to be, absent an embrace of their own eternal present. Camus explicitly compares Sisyphus to the modern worker: "The workman of today works every day in his life at the same tasks, and this fate is no less absurd."[122]

While Camus described some of the trickery in which Sisyphus engaged at the beginning of his essay, these anecdotes are told a bit differently elsewhere, and Sisyphus is called a Trickster.[123] To what extent this nuance

---

[121] *Id.* at p. 91.

[122] *Id.* at p. 90.

[123] *See, e.g.,* The Editors of Encyclopaedia Britannica, revised and updated by Jeff Wallenfeldt, "Sisyphus," *Encyclopædia Britannica* (Encyclopædia Britannica, Inc., July 10, 2020), https://www.britannica.com/topic/Sisyphus.

informs Camus' retelling of the story is up to the reader. Were the reader to decide that the Trickster archetype is indeed a part of Camus' essay, moreover, it then becomes another decision as to whether only people who can adopt the outlook of the Trickster can embrace pointless labor.

In either case, "The Myth of Sisyphus" shows that it is possible for one to not be philosophically defeated by unrewarding labor. That one is not philosophically defeated, however, does not make some unrewarding labor any less physically tiring. In "Breathe Reprise," it is a *cold and tired* man that looks up to hear the sound of far-away church bells in the second verse. We do not know what has made him tired, but whatever that labor is, he is inured to it.

The bells he hears from across the fields in "Breathe Reprise" are not simply noting the time, as would be the case in "Time." They are more likely to be a call to a service about to begin (*Calls the faithful to their knees*). It also could be, however, something like the Angelus bells of the Roman Catholic and some Anglican and Lutheran Churches, a call to pray and spread goodwill to everyone on Earth, which did not need to be practiced in an actual church.[124]

Though we have determined that our hero is not suffering from existential angst, it nonetheless seems equally unlikely that he is experiencing Angelus joy, given the lonely distance from which the sound comes. Instead, the evocation is of something ancient suggested by the bells being made of iron, like early Christian bells made of hammered and riveted iron plates,[125] and the listeners being brought to their knees by magic.

Possibly it is closer to the Edgar Allen Poe 1849 poem, "The Bells:"[126]

Hear the tolling of the bells,

Iron bells!

What a world of solemn thought their monody compels!

In this context, it seems that Poe is using monody in the sense of a solo song, though its other meanings — as an ode in a Greek tragedy or a lament over someone's death — add a deep resonance to the word. Poe's iron bells go on to become overtly threatening, moreover:[127]

In the silence of the night

How we shiver with affright

---

[124] "Glossary of Roman Catholic Church Terms, Words and Phrases," CatholicIreland.net (The Church Support Group), accessed November 23, 2020, https://www.catholicireland.net/glossary-of-terms.

[125] Blagovest Bells, "What Is a Bell?," (Blagovest Bells/Expanding Edge LLC), accessed October 13, 2020, http://www.russianbells.com/acoustics/what-is-bell.html.

[126] Edgar Allan Poe, "The Bells," Internet Archive (Philadelphia, Porter & Coates/Library of Congress, November 18, 2010), https://archive.org/details/bells00poee, p. 44.

[127] Id., p. 45.

At the melancholy menace of their tone!

It is unlikely that our tired hero would rest himself beside a fire were there bells chiming menace into the night, so Poe's bells also seem unlikely to be the bells in "Breathe Reprise." Breathe Reprise" is not about a clash with present peril. Coming after the songs "Breathe" and "Time," however, "Breathe Reprise" may reflect a weariness after battling the world. It is like "His Epitaph," written by Stephen Hawes, who himself rested in 1523:[128]

O MORTAL folk, you may behold and see

How I lie here, sometime a mighty knight:

The end of joy and all prosperitee

Is death at last, thorough his course and might:

After the day there cometh the dark night,

For though the daye be never so long,

At last the bells ringeth to evensong.

Lingering by the Sea

By warming his bones beside the fire, the hero of "Breathe Reprise" may be preparing himself for his own dark night, a time when bells may peal and he can no longer hear them. It is as in the famous Sea-nymphs' knell in Ariel's song to Ferdinand, in Shakespeare's *Midsummer Night's Dream*:

Full fathom five thy father lies;

Of his bones are coral made;

Those are pearls that were his eyes:

Nothing of him that doth fade,

But doth suffer a sea-change

Into something rich and strange.

Sea-nymphs hourly ring his knell:

Ding-dong.

Hark! now I hear them—Ding-dong, bell.[129]

This song is sung by the magical sprite Ariel to the recently shipwrecked Prince Ferdinand of Naples, who erroneously believes his father has drowned in the five-fathom-deep water. Ariel is invisible to Ferdinand, and Ferdinand

---

[128] Stephen Hawes, "His Epitaph," in Sherman Ripley, ed., "Beyond : an Anthology of Immortality," Internet Archive (D. Appleton and Company, New York / State Library of Pennsylvania, January 1, 1970), https://archive.org/details/beyondanthologyo00unse, p. 62.

[129] W. Shakespeare, "The Tempest" in *The Yale Shakespeare*, p. 1412 (I, ii, 464-473).

is drawn to the song, which assuages his grief somewhat. It enables him to imagine his father's death was not meaningless, and that his body has not decayed but has instead been turned into something precious and beautiful, of pearls and coral, which is celebrated by sea-nymphs with tolling bells.

In "Breathe Reprise," however, though bells may sound, they do not call to our hero but to the faithful. This is reminiscent of T. S. Eliot's Prufrock, whom we encountered first evoked in the song "Time." Unlike Ariel's song to Ferdinand, though Prufrock may hear the voices from the sea, they are nonetheless not intended for his ears, and though he may dream of mermaids, they remain only dreams. His reality is much more mundane:

24. 1918 illustration by Louis Rhead of *The Tempest* in *Tales from Shakespeare*, Charles Lamb and Mary Lamb, "Tales from Shakespeare," illustr. Louis Rhead, Internet Archive (Harper & Bros, New York, London/University of North Carolina at Chapel Hill, March 19, 2012), https://archive.org/details/talesfromshakesplamb.

I have heard the mermaids singing, each to each.

I do not think that they will sing to me.

I have seen them riding seaward on the waves

Combing the white hair of the waves blown back

When the wind blows the water white and black.

We have lingered in the chambers of the sea

By sea-girls wreathed with seaweed red and brown

Till human voices wake us, and we drown.[130]

Eliot uses drowning to remind us that all the adventure and toil in life may have no meaning once that life is ended (as Ferdinand believed would be the fate of his father). Eliot emphasized this lesson in "Death By Water," the shortest and most formal segment of his masterpiece, *The Wasteland*:

Phlebas the Phoenician, a fortnight dead,

Forgot the cry of gulls, and the deep seas swell

And the profit and loss.

    A current under sea

Picked his bones in whispers. As he rose and fell

He passed the stages of his age and youth

Entering the whirlpool.

    Gentile or Jew

O you who turn the wheel and look to windward,

Consider Phlebas, who was once handsome and tall as you.[131]

As described in an article by Christopher Ricks and Jim McCue, these lines were all that were left after editing by Ezra Pound — whom Eliot called the better craftsman in the poem's dedication — from the original 93 lines.[132] Pound insisted that the lines about Phlebas remain, even though they were a tightened translation of a poem Eliot had published in French, "Dans le Restaurant," only a couple years before.[133]

"Consider Phlebas, who was once handsome and tall as you" is not so much a warning, or even a caution, but a cold reminder of the vanity of notions of accomplishment. This reminder goes back centuries, even to Ecclesiastes again, which had first been evoked in "Time:"

All things are full of weariness;

---

[130] T. S. Eliot, "Prufrock and Other Observations," p. 42.

[131] T. S. Eliot, "The Waste Land, 1922 First Edition of the Book and Poem by T. S. Eliot," ed. Wikisource contributors, Wikisource, the free online library (Wikimedia Foundation, Inc., July 19, 2018), https://en.wikisource.org/w/index.php?title=The_Waste_Land, lines 312-21.

[132] Jim McCue and Christopher Ricks, "Masterpiece in the Making — Poetry," TLS (The Times Literary Supplement Limited, November 2015), https://www.the-tls.co.uk/articles/masterpiece-in-the-making. McCue and Ricks are the editors of the two-volume *The Poems of T. S. Eliot*.

[133] *Id*.

a man cannot utter it;

the eye is not satisfied with seeing,

nor the ear filled with hearing.

What has been is what will be,

and what has been done is what will be done,

and there is nothing new under the sun.

Is there a thing of which it is said,

"See, this is new"?

It has been already

in the ages before us.

There is no remembrance of former things,

nor will there be any remembrance

of later things yet to be

among those who come after. [134]

But the hero of "Breathe Reprise" is tired to the bone, and does not appear concerned with any of this. His work is done and he can rest, drawing warmth from the fire and abstract, secular comfort from the faraway church bells. He is not drawn to those bells; no promise of some sweet hereafter beckons to him. That is for the faithful, among whom he does not count himself.

Nor is it clear that our hero would want to be counted among the faithful. Though the wearying paths of the life reflected in the songs in the album thus far may have worn out the hero, he does not seem to have reached the point where he wishes now to be told what to do. This is what he thinks it is to be called to your knees.

The faithful are called to kneel, to accept what they can of the magic spells they hear. For the faithful, there is no self or choices, only surrender and submission. This surrender is borne out by the fall of the synthesizer, which evokes an organ in church, to silence at the end of "Breathe Reprise." All other instruments had faded moments before, leaving only the sepulchral organ sound.

But to surrender is a choice as well, and to be effective as a choice requires a great deal of courage from the person who would so choose. As Kierkeg-aard had stated in *Fear and Trembling*, his penetrating analysis of the biblical story of how God demanded that Abraham sacrifice his son Isaac, "A purely

---

[134] Eccl 8-11.

human courage is required to renounce the whole of the temporal to gain the eternal . . ."[135]

To Kierkegaard, Abraham had no reason other than faith to perform such an apparently abominable act. Kierkegaard believed completely that to have such faith meant and required that God's will transcended any human ethics or reason. As Jesus Christ had said, God's plans reach into even the finest detail of life:[136]

> Are not two sparrows sold for a penny? And not one of them will fall to the ground apart from your Father. But even the hairs of your head are all numbered.

Though God's plans were so comprehensive, when challenged about seemingly arbitrary, terrible things that happened to apparently innocent people, Jesus warned the people not to think that this was for any reason that they could fathom:[137]

> Or those eighteen on whom the tower in Siloam fell and killed them: do you think that they were worse offenders than all the others who lived in Jerusalem? No, I tell you; but unless you repent, you will all likewise perish.

Though this rule may appear harsh, as Kierkegaard had insisted, utter and complete surrender is required. In that, Kierkegaard's rigor is much as Jesus Christ described:[138]

> And behold, a man came up to him, saying, "Teacher, what good deed must I do to have eternal life?" And he said to him, "Why do you ask me about what is good? There is only one who is good. If you would enter life, keep the commandments." He said to him, "Which ones?" And Jesus said, "You shall not murder, You shall not commit adultery, You shall not steal, You shall not bear false witness, Honor your father and mother, and, You shall love your neighbor as yourself." The young man said to him, "All these I have kept. What do I still lack?" Jesus said to him, "If you would be perfect, go, sell what you possess and give to the poor, and you will have treasure in heaven; and come, follow me." When the young man heard this he went away sorrowful, for he had great possessions.

---

[135] Søren Kierkegaard, *Fear and Trembling*, p. 21.

[136] Matt 10: 29-31, "Bible Gateway Passage: Matthew 10:29-31 — English Standard Version," Bible Gateway (Crossway Bibles, a publishing ministry of Good News Publishers), accessed October 16, 2020, https://www.biblegateway.com/passage/?search=Matthew+10%3A29-31&version=ESV.

[137] Luke 13: 4-5, "Bible Gateway Passage: Luke 13:4-5 — English Standard Version," Bible Gateway (Crossway Bibles, a publishing ministry of Good News Publishers), accessed October 16, 2020, https://www.biblegateway.com/passage/?search=Luke+13&version=ESV.

[138] Matt 19: 16-30.

While this is a tremendous sacrifice, for those who can submit, the reward can be great. Not counting the promise of heaven so many religions provide, in surrender many people find actual worldly rewards in the here and now. As described by William James, who has been referred to as the father of American psychology,[139] the decision to surrender to faith is indeed enormous, and wreaks a sea-change in the person's life:[140]

> Under these circumstances the way to success, as vouched for by innumerable authentic personal narrations, is by an anti-moralistic method, by the "surrender" of which I spoke in my second lecture. Passivity, not activity; relaxation, not intentness, should be now the rule. Give up the feeling of responsibility, let go your hold, resign the care of your destiny to higher powers, be genuinely indifferent as to what becomes of it all, and you will find not only that you gain a perfect inward relief, but often also, in addition, the particular goods you sincerely thought you were renouncing. This is the salvation through self-despair, the dying to be truly born, of Lutheran theology, the passage into *nothing* of which Jacob Behmen writes. To get to it, a critical point must usually be passed, a corner turned within one. Something must give way, a native hardness must break down and liquefy; and this event (as we shall abundantly see hereafter) is frequently sudden and automatic, and leaves on the Subject an impression that he has been wrought on by an external power.

The Jacob Behmen (also called Jakob Böhme and Jacob Boehme) to whom William James refers was a very influential 17th century religious mystic and theologian.[141] After his marriage and setting up shop as a shoemaker, Böhme experienced visions that prompted him to write about the importance of individual faith, and how God's knowledge of Himself was revealed through His creation.[142] Böhme influenced a large number of important modern religious, philosophical, and psychological figures, including Georg Wilhelm Friedrich Hegel, Friedrich Nietzsche, Martin Heidegger, and Carl Jung.[143]

---

[139] In lectures collected and first published in 1902 as *The Varieties of Religious Experience.* *See* Kendra Cherry, "The Life and Theories of Psychologist William James," Verywell Mind (About, Inc. [Dotdash], April 23, 2020), http://psychology.about.com/od/profilesofmajorthinkers/p/jamesbio.htm.

[140] William James and Reinhold Niebuhr, *The Varieties of Religious Experience: a Study in Human Nature; with a New Introd. by Reinhold Niebuhr*, intro. Reinhold Niebuhr (New York: Simon & Schuster, 1997), p. 101. An online version may be found at https://archive.org/download/varietiesreligi03jamegoog/varietiesreligi03jamegoog.pdf.

[141] Kathleen O'Bannon, "Jacob Behmen, An Appreciation, by Alexander Whyte," Christian Classics Ethereal Library (Harry Plantinga), accessed November 23, 2020, https://www.ccel.org/ccel/whyte/behmen.html.

[142] "Jakob Böhme," Jakob Böhme — New World Encyclopedia (Paragon House Publishers), accessed October 18, 2020, https://www.newworldencyclopedia.org/entry/Jakob_Böhme.

[143] *Id.*

William James goes on in the paragraph following that quoted above to say that this surrender is one of the fundamental forms of human experience, and its consequences are profound: "Some say that the capacity or incapacity for it is what divides the religious from the merely moralistic character."[144] That is, the hero of "Breathe Reprise" may have been constitutionally unable to surrender to faith, whether or not he wished to.

Taking a somewhat different tack than Kierkegaard about the obscurity of God's will, James says that simply because being religious does not necessarily make rational sense is no reason at all to reject it:[145]

> Nevertheless, if we look on man's whole mental life as it exists, on the life of men that lies in them apart from their learning and science, and that they inwardly and privately follow, we have to confess that the part of it of which rationalism can give an account is relatively superficial. It is the part that has the prestige undoubtedly, for it has the loquacity, it can challenge you for proofs, and chop logic, and put you down with words. But it will fail to convince or convert you all the same, if your dumb intuitions are opposed to its conclusions. If you have intuitions at all, they come from a deeper level of your nature than the loquacious level which rationalism inhabits. Your whole subconscious life, your impulses, your faiths, your needs, your divinations, have prepared the premises, of which your consciousness now feels the weight of the result; and something in you absolutely knows that that result must be truer than any logic-chopping rationalistic talk, however clever, that may contradict it.

While some may infer pejorative meanings to both the phrases *to their knees* and *magic spells*, there does not appear to be anything intrinsically judgmental about "Breathe Reprise." As we have seen from these passages from William James, submission is not in itself necessarily a negative, hence to be on one's knees is no deficiency. Similarly, to many, many people, the idea of magic as a powerful force that can bring them something beyond themselves is a comforting thought.

Moreover, it may be said that magic spells were very important to some surprising individuals, people who may have been counted among the logic-chopping rationalists in history. It is probably not surprising that Tycho Brahe and Galileo practiced astrology, because this practice does follow and depend on the positions of astrological objects.

A less obvious example, however, is Isaac Newton, who is often thought of the father of modern science. Though Newton created calculus and worked out the laws of gravity that lasted essentially unmodified until Einstein, Newton also wrote extensively on alchemy, prompting the famous econo-

---

[144] William James, *The Varieties of Religious Experience*, at pp. 101–102.
[145] *Id.* at p. 74.

mist John Maynard Keynes to name him "the last of the magicians."[146] An entire section of The Newton Project — which seeks to make all of Newton's works publicly available — is devoted to his alchemical studies.[147]

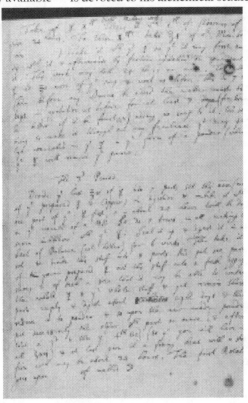

25. Isaac Newton's notes on the manufacture of the Philosopher's Stone, to turn base metals into gold. This image is courtesy the Othmer Library of Chemical History, at the Science History Institute, and may be found at Wikimedia Commons as part of a cooperation project.

Though most people today take the notion of alchemy as magic, this may be a misjudgment. Some argue strongly that the present magical connotation of alchemy is a relatively recent interpretation, and that Newton himself would not have seen alchemy as anything but chemistry. For example, Lawrence M. Principe of Johns Hopkins University argued in his essay, "Reflections on Newton's Alchemy in Light of the New Historiography of

[146] "Sir Isaac Newton: Magician's Brain," *The Economist* (The Economist Newspaper, June 19, 2014), https://www.economist.com/books-and-arts/2014/06/19/magicians-brain.

[147] "Introducing Newton's Alchemical Papers" (The Newton Project), accessed October 18, 2020, http://www.newtonproject.ox.ac.uk/texts/newtons-works/alchemical.

Alchemy,"[148] that Newton's work should indeed be considered chemistry, inasmuch as the occult connotations of alchemy were a product of the 1800s, well more than a hundred years after Newton had done his experimentation.

Accordingly, just as we must not be too quick to judge Newton for his alchemy, we must be careful in our consideration of the phrases *to their knees* and *magic spells*. If there were any judgment to be inferred, moreover, the structure of the album suggests it should be positive: Even as the organ falls to silence in "Breathe Reprise," a solo piano has begun playing.

This is the beginning of "The Great Gig in the Sky," which contains one of the most famous soaring vocal solos in rock music. Coming just after "Breathe Reprise," it seems to represent a fervent embrace of magic spells, although not much of it would ever be called *softly spoken*.

Track Six: The Great Gig in the Sky

Rick Wright's beautiful solo piano introduction to "The Great Gig in the Sky" sets a moody, even elegiac, pace and tone, evoking feelings that are ancient and mysterious. It is not unlike the familiar first movement of Beethoven's "Moonlight Sonata."[149] About 17 seconds into "The Great Gig in the Sky," slide guitar and bass join the piano, making a fuller, yet still restful, sound. After another 20 or so seconds, an older man's voice observes:

And I am not frightened of dying. Any time will do, I don't mind.

Why should I be frightened of dying? There's no reason for it. You've gotta go some-time.[150]

These spoken words could well be those of the hero from "Breathe Reprise," as he warms his bones beside the fire. He neither fears nor joyfully anticipates death; death is not something he dwells upon, any more than he dwells upon where or what he was before he was born. Whatever has gone on in his life, he is reconciled to its finite beginning and — sooner or later — finite end. Without an expectation of punishment or reward beyond this life, he is at peace.

But those sentiments were from "Breathe Reprise," not "The Great Gig in the Sky."

Moments after the words of the older man have ceased, cymbals begin to beat the time quietly for a moment or two, but then the whole drum kit

---

[148] Lawrence M. Principe, "Reflections on Newton's Alchemy in Light of the New Historiography of Alchemy,'" in *Newton and Newtonianism: New Studies*, ed. James E. Force and Sarah Hutton (Dordrecht: Kluwer Academic Publishers, 2004), pp. 209–11.

[149] Ludwig van Beethoven, *Piano Sonata No. 14 in C-sharp minor*, "Quasi una fantasia," Op. 27, No. 2.

[150] Kit Rae, "Dark Side of the Moon Bootleg Soundclips and Other Stuff."

is engaged as Clare Torry's voice soars into her iconic "Great Gig in the Sky" solo.

The solo is wordless and soaring, breathy and bluesy, as much gospel music as orgasm. It is much too sensual to be a hymn, though you might have expected such from the reference to the faithful on their knees in "Breathe Reprise." It is not at all a stretch to characterize this vocal solo as a magic spell.

The solo is an overflowing, powerful dance with the accompanying music, creating a world only hinted at by the melody. It gives the sense of a journey from one sonic, psychic, emotional level to another, untethered and undescribable by the usual Rock sensibilities. Full-throated outpourings are coupled with hoarse calls, wailing and shrieking. It is more an opera aria — soaring like "Il dolce suono" from Gaetano Donizetti's *Lucia de Lammermoor*[151]— than what you expect from backup singing.

This solo came about in a way in keeping with other aspects of the album: a strong central idea, coupled to enormous synchronicity.

The primary ideas for "The Great Gig in the Sky" had been well established for many months, but did not have anyone singing. The band was already performing a version of the album in concert halls and stadiums, with its first — albeit incomplete — debut on January 20, 1972, at the Brighton Dome in England and a second, successful, performance the next night in Portsmouth, more than a year before the album release.[152]

On *Pink Floyd Crackers (Damn Braces: Bless Relaxes)* — *The Entire 1972 Hollywood Bowl Concert*, a 1976 unofficial vinyl bootleg release of the September 22, 1972 concert, the entirety of the early album can be found. That said, because of its unofficial nature, this vinyl version may be difficult to obtain. For example, on the massive marketplace for vinyl Discogs, trading in *Crackers* is expressly prohibited: "This release has been blocked from sale in the marketplace. It is not permitted to sell this item on Discogs."[153]

While most of the *The Dark Side of the Moon* material on *Crackers* is familiar in tempo and internal arrangement, some differences are obvious. For example, "On the Run" is quite jaunty, with bouncy guitar and bass, and none of the effects that create the narrative on the studio recording.

---

[151] Gaetano Donizetti, "Il dolce suono," *Lucia de Lammermoor*.

[152] Bryan Wawzenek, "When Pink Floyd Flubbed Live Debut of 'The Dark Side of the Moon'," Ultimate Classic Rock (Ultimate Classic Rock, March 2, 2018), http://ultimate-classicrock.com/pink-floyd-live-debut-dark-side/.

[153] "Pink Floyd — Crackers (Damn Braces: Bless Relaxes) The Entire 1972 Hollywood Bowl Concert," Discogs (Discogs, January 1, 1976), https://www.discogs.com/Pink-Floyd-Crackers-Damn-Braces-Bless-Relaxes-The-Entire-1972-Hollywood-Bowl-Concert/release/1135332.

Most notable, however, is the presentation of "Breathe Reprise," which feels fundamentally different with no vocals. This version begins with piano and organ, which are joined eventually by drums and bass. There is a hard-to-understand spoken track underpinning the early part of the song. It is not clear whether this was intended by Pink Floyd, or was an artifact of the *ad hoc* bootleg recording process. Where Clare Torry would have begun her solo, however, there is simply a prominent bass line walked forward. Guitar is then added. After an instrumental jam, the song returns to Rick Wright's piano and hymn-like keyboards until it fades. As it is fading, moreover, the cash register sound effects of "Money" commence, without any break.

Another early version of the album is found on a recording of the March 13, 1972 concert in Sapporo, Japan.[154] Many of *The Dark Side of the Moon* songs in this concert recording also differ in varying degrees from what ultimately found its way to the studio album. While most are recognizable as earlier versions of those now-familiar songs, these versions of "The Great Gig in the Sky" lack the soaring aspects of the studio version. The Sapporo recording does have the solemn, sepulchral, quality of much of the studio version, however, and has some keyboard excursions reminiscent of "Echoes," on the *Meddle* album. Without the singing, though, it has an entirely different feeling; it is a very different song.

Of course, the familiar, uniquely inspiring version that is on the studio release inescapably colors any interpretation of the previous 1972 live versions. It is nonetheless evident from those earlier efforts that Pink Floyd as a group was still groping for an adequate completion to what seemed a work in progress.

26. The vinyl bootleg recording *Pink Floyd Crackers (Damn Braces: Bless Relaxes) — The Entire 1972 Hollywood Bowl Concert* album was released in 1976. Cover photographs courtesy the author.

Moving from the instrumental live versions like those mentioned above to an early studio mix from 1972 found on Disc 6 of *The Dark Side of the Moon Immersion Box Set*, the band can be heard experimenting by inserting a monologue from Apollo 17 astronaut Gene Cernan, recorded during an actual

---

[154] "Pink Floyd Live March 13, 1972," Internet Archive (isladeencanto12, March 16, 2016), https://archive.org/details/pf_1972-03-13_04/REC 1 — Brain Damage unedited.flac. No Creative Commons License is immediately discernible for this recording.

manned trip to the moon.[155] This studio mix was prepared in December 1972, only a matter of weeks after the September 22, 1972, Hollywood Bowl concert.

The astronaut recording on this version "The Great Gig in the Sky" has the harsh, crackly, low-fidelity voice communications familiar to the 1970s audiences from broadcasts of the Apollo program. The sound is jarring and grating in comparison to the smoothness of the rest of the album. Even the background announcement in "On the Run," though difficult to understand because of its relative quiet compared to the synthesizers and drum, is nonetheless static-free and as distinct as its volume allows.

The astronaut effect may have been a throwback to "Astronomy Domine," the from 1967 album *The Piper at the Gates of Dawn*, in which Pink Floyd's then-manager speaks through a megaphone to make a distorted emulation of astronaut radio communication.[156]

The Moment Matters

This astronaut voice-over did not seem to fit the Rick Wright composition, however, and the band kept their minds open to possible paths. What ultimately brought the song to its integrated studio form was the result of looking outside the four walls of the Abbey Road Studio and the four members of the band, looking instead for what the world outside had to offer.

As described by Clare Torry, a British singer Alan Parsons knew from her covers of popular songs, Torry received a call when Pink Floyd was nearly finished with the studio album, but were still casting about for closure. The band had not yet even given the song a settled title, and they gave her no strong direction other than to not use actual words.

After her initial *ooo-baby*-type vocalizing was rejected, she decided to pretend to be an instrument — a saxophone or string quartet. Two complete takes were recorded. She stopped during the third, thinking she had already done her best by then.

Ms. Torry emphasized that her first two takes were the most important, as they were from an unrestrained place within herself. She could tell from the beginning of the third take that she was starting to think consciously of the melodic lines rather than having them come to her spontaneously. She

[155] Cap Blackard, "What's in the Box!?: Pink Floyd — The Dark Side of the Moon Immersion Box Set," Consequence of Sound (Consequence of Sound, December 9, 2011), http://consequenceofsound.net/2011/12/whats-in-the-box-pink-floyd-the-dark-side-of-the-moon-immersion-box-set.

[156] Ennio Gallucci, "Who Sang the Most Pink Floyd Songs? Lead Vocal Totals," Ultimate Classic Rock (Ultimate Classic Rock, March 20, 2020), https://ultimateclassicrock.com/pink-floyd-lead-vocals-songs.

realized it was becoming repetitive and contrived, and so she told them they had enough.[157]

27. This photograph of Gene Cernan, taken by fellow Apollo 17 astronaut Harrison Schmitt in the Taurus—Littrow Valley of the Moon, on December 12, 1972, is courtesy National Aeronautics and Space Administration. https://www.hq.nasa.gov/alsj/a17/AS17-140-21391.jpg.

Ms. Torry describes the fortuity of it all:[158]

How did it happen? Umm . . . who knows? I've often wondered. Because it's given me some grief over the years. I've often wondered if it was the devil grinning up at me or god smiling down at me. And I still haven't figured out which one had the final say.

---

[157] Russell Reising, 'Speak to Me': the Legacy of Pink Floyd's The Dark Side of the Moon (Aldershot: Ashgate, 2005), page 151.

[158] Mark Deutsch, "Clare Torry: Her Greatest Gig. The One She Almost Skipped," Clare Torry: Her greatest gig. The one she almost skipped, March 2013, http://markdeutsch39.blogspot.com/2013/03/clare-torry-her-greatest-gig-one-she.html.

Ms. Torry's intuitive response to Rick Wright's composition can be thought of as pushing herself beyond what she had experienced and incorporated into herself, into a new place, a new self. As Torry herself put it:[159]

> But I have to say the one thing I said to my boyfriend at the time after I had done it, I never thought I could sing that high — and that's what excited me — but I honestly, truthfully, never thought it would see the light of day. I thought they'd just say, 'Thank you very much,' and really you could have knocked me down with a feather when it was released.

This interview excerpt illustrates how important creative moments may not be recognized when they take place, even by their creator. That is, when Clare Torry left the Abbey Road studio after her couple of takes, she knew that they were outside the norm of accompaniments, and was very doubtful that her vocals would be used in the final production of *The Dark Side Of The Moon* recording. She later said that the only way she knew it was used was when she actually saw the record in a record store, picked it up and found her name in the credits.[160]

In some ways, Clare Torry's tremendous performance is similar to another fortuitous occurrence associated with remarkable vocals. When one thinks of very moving vocal soarings in rock music, it is only a few moments before the female accompaniment to the Rolling Stones' "Gimme Shelter" comes to mind. As Mick Jagger recounts, soul singer Merry Clayton's powerful background vocals came about in the almost spontaneous way that Clare Torry's did:[161]

> When we got to Los Angeles and we were mixing it, we thought, 'Well, it'd be great to have a woman come and do the rape/murder verse,' or chorus or whatever you want to call it," said Jagger. "We randomly phoned up this poor lady in the middle of the night, and she arrived in her curlers and proceeded to do that in one or two takes, which is pretty amazing. She came in and knocked off this rather odd lyric. It's not the sort of lyric you give anyone—'Rape, murder/It's just a shot away'—but she really got into it, as you can hear on the record.

How surprised and impressed the Rolling Stones were by Ms. Clayton's performance is reflected on the recording itself: At approximately three minutes into the song, if you listen very carefully, you can hear a spontaneous shout from someone in the studio in reaction to the performance. While

---

[159] *Id.*

[160] *Id.*

[161] NPR Staff, "Mick Jagger On The Apocalyptic 'Gimme Shelter'," NPR (NPR, November 16, 2012), https://www.npr.org/2012/11/16/165270769/mick-jagger-on-the-apocalyptic-gimme-shelter.

another take could have been made without the shout from the gallery, it would not have been the same.

The power of the synchronistic moment of that original recording session cannot be denied, but its absence makes a telling difference: Merry Clayton's own subsequent cover of the song "Gimme Shelter"[162] does not have the same raw, tortured, strained, screaming quality of the original. It is a strong cover, certainly, but it does not give you goosebumps like the original.

That Clare Torry's vocals on "The Great Gig in the Sky" were without words, on the other hand, seems critical to what became the final album and subsequent performance version. The mystical, solemn, religious feeling engendered by Rick Wright's chords is deeply felt, stirring things that would likely be diminished by anything but the most profound of lyrics, lyrics which had not begun to take roots even after many months of touring with the song.

Such non-verbal vocals, or non-lexical vocables, were very much in the air in rock music in the late 1960s and early 1970s. For example, "Child in Time" by Deep Purple, on the 1970 album *Deep Purple In Rock*, was an emotional protest against the nuclear threat, recorded at the height of the Cold War.[163] What would have been a brooding song is given much more energy and depth by Ian Gillan's soaring cries. While the studio version on *In Rock* is excellent, an even more emotional rendition is found on the 1972 live album *Made In Japan*. In this concert setting, Gillan's vocals on "Child in Time" are much like his in the aria "I Only Want to Say (Gethsemane)" in the 1970 rock opera *Jesus Christ Superstar*, in which Gillan plays Jesus. As in "The Great Gig in the Sky," these non-verbal flights of voice bring goosebumps.

Even the most popular band of the time period, The Beatles, had utilized non-verbal segments in many of their biggest hits. The song "Hey Jude," issued in 1968 as the first single on The Beatles' own Apple Records label,[164] is very well known for its *Na-na-na-na* bridge. If you listen very carefully, and with an open mind, Paul McCartney's *Yeah-yeah-yeah-yeah* break at approximately 6:09 to 6:18 in "Hey Jude" is very like Clare Torry's at 1:41 to 1:46 in "The Great Gig in the Sky."

It is not too far-fetched to imagine that McCartney's vocals were echoing inside Clare Torry, moreover. While the single of "Hey Jude" had spent many

[162] Merry Clayton, "Merry Clayton — Gimme Shelter," Internet Archive, September 1, 2011, https://archive.org/details/MerryClayton-GimmeShelter.

[163] Ian Gillan, "Ian Comments on the Words of Some Songs in His Life — 16 'Child in Time'," Caramba!-Wordography, accessed October 31, 2020, http://www.gillan.com/wordography-16.html.

[164] Richard Havers, "The Successful Launch Of Apple Records: UDiscover," uDiscover Music (Universal Music Operations Limited, August 26, 2020), https://www.udiscover-music.com/stories/d-day-for-apple-records.

weeks on the charts in 1968, it re-entered the popular ear through heavy airplay again in early 1970, with the release of the compilation album called *Hey Jude*.[165]

Ms. Torry's excitement at reaching a new peak in her life is an ironic aspect of "The Great Gig in the Sky." When Rick Wright composed the music to which Ms. Torry had such a vivid response, he was very much suffused with a palpable fear of death. In the March 1998 issue of the magazine *Mojo*, Wright described "The Great Gig in the Sky" in somewhat dark terms, inasmuch as he was in constant fear of dying, with all of the air and highway travel. That the second half of the song is more gentle is because the dying person has stopped fighting and begun fading.[166]

But the influence of Clare Torry's vocal on Wright could ultimately be thought of as almost magical, as it changed entirely the manner in which he described his own composition:[167]

> I didn't, when I wrote it, think, 'This is all about death,' cos I don't think I would have written that chord structure. I get so excited when I hear Clare singing. For me, it's not necessarily death. I hear terror and fear and huge emotion, in the middle bit especially, and the way the voice blends with the band.

At the very end of the side, as the music is finally fading, there are perceptible changes in pitch. There is no obvious reason for these shifts. It is, though, one last element of slipping outside what is expected to reinforce the nonlinearity of the landscape that comprehends "Speak to Me," "Breathe," "On the Run," "Time," "Breathe Reprise," and "The Great Gig in the Sky."

And so instruments and voice come to an ethereal end, closing "The Great Gig in the Sky" and ending Side One of *The Dark Side of the Moon*.

---

[165] Dave Lifton, "When the Beatles Cleaned Out Their Closet for the 'Hey Jude' LP," Ultimate Classic Rock (Ultimate Classic Rock, Townsquare Media, Inc., February 26, 2016), https://ultimateclassicrock.com/beatles-hey-jude-album.

[166] Matthew Kitchen, "What Is Pink Floyd's Dark Side of the Moon Really About? An Introduction.," *Esquire* (Hearst Magazine Media, Inc., March 26, 2013), https://www.esquire.com/entertainment/music/a17945/what-is-dark-side-of-the-moon-about-15266894.

[167] Id.

SIDE TWO

It is difficult to explain to people that only know of *The Dark Side of the Moon* through streaming, digital downloads, or CDs, how important the difference with vinyl really is. Though people may argue about the smoother, richer, or less brittle sound of analogue recordings, there is one point that is not open to debate: Changing the sides of a vinyl record is a necessary pause in the performance, a quiet moment in which one cannot but reflect at some level on what one has just heard.

In the case of *The Dark Side of the Moon*, even though each song of Side One merged into the next, everything stopped after the last contemplative moments of "The Great Gig in the Sky" faded. The listener may thus fall into a brief reverie, linger for a moment in some mental meadow of their very own. Full of deep thoughts, conscious or not, the listener puts on Side Two and is jolted right out of them with the cash-register clang that heralds the start of "Money."

28. This photograph of Side Two of *The Dark Side of the Moon* on the turntable was taken by the author.

Track Seven: Money

The characteristic bell of a cash register, the sound of the gathering of change out of the cash register drawer, and the tearing of a paper register tape begin "Money." Rather, sound effects for each, as opposed to an actual retail transaction. For example, the sound of change is that of Roger Waters throwing coins into one of his wife's mixing bowls.[168] The bell/change/tape pattern repeats itself without any conventional musical accompaniment for ten or twelve seconds, establishing a distinctive rhythm before the iconic bass line begins.

These rhythmic cash register sounds from "Money" have been sampled and used innumerable times, appearing on radio, television, or whenever the idea of commerce needs to be suggested. Though this set of sounds was ubiquitous for many decades and familiar to anyone who had ever gone grocery shopping, it has long since passed into retail history almost everywhere. There well may be millions of listeners who have never heard the sounds of a cash register bell outside of the song "Money" or someone sampling the song "Money."

29. This cash register photograph, taken July 10, 1957, by Warren K. Leffler, is now in the U.S. News & World Report Magazine Photograph Collection in the Library of Congress. https://www.loc.gov/item/2017657574/.

---

[168] Neil Cossar, "The Great Gig In The Sky," This Day In Music, March 4, 2020, https://www.thisdayinmusic.com/liner-notes/the-great-gig-in-the-sky/.

After setting the distinctive tempo, which is joined by a bass guitar, these cash register sounds fade away after about forty seconds, though returning between the first and second verse, at about 1:18.

It is the bass line that stands out, however, really grabbing the listener's attention. While the cash register sounds are novel, the bass riff stands out from other rock music. The progression was thought up by Roger Waters, with an unusual 7/4 time signature.[169] At the time, the 7/4 time could not be found in any other familiar popular song. This time signature would be used a few years later in another hit, Peter Gabriel's 1977 single *Solsbury Hill*.[170]

The chords in "Money" are simple and catchy, making it easy to find yourself humming *dum dum de dum dum dum dum dum* to yourself. The song could easily fit into a Classic Rock block with the Beatles' "Obladi Oblada" or Paul Simon's "Kodachrome." While "Obladi Oblada" and "Kodachrome" both have lighthearted, tongue-in-cheek, ironic qualities to accompany their poppy beat, though, the lyrics of "Money" go beyond plain irony into biting, sardonic, cynical satire.

Interestingly, there was another hit song in the early Seventies about money, "(For the Love of) Money," by the O'Jays, which also began with a very distinctive bass line. "(For the Love of) Money" is unironic and unambiguous in its rejection and condemnation of the high life. Pink Floyd's "Money," in contrast, for all its angst, sarcasm, and contempt, is not so clear in how it ultimately comes out on the issue of being rich.

The lyrics of "Money" start with a feeling familiar to many, the relief of being regularly employed and finally having enough money after paying bills to put some in the bank:

> *Money, get away.*
> *Get a good job with more pay and you're O. K.*
> *Money, it's a gas.*
> *Grab that cash with both hands and make a stash.*

While this initial feeling might be familiar to most listeners, "Money" then turns immediately fanciful and extravagant, celebrating indulgences rarely shared by the common listener:

> *New car, caviar, four star daydream,*
> *Think I'll buy me a football team.*

[169]Far Out Staff, "Hear Pink Floyd Gem 'Money' through Roger Waters' Isolated Bass Track," *Far Out Magazine*, August 7, 2020, https://faroutmagazine.co.uk/roger-waters-pink-floyd-money-isolated-bass-track.

[170]Andrew Unterberger, "10 Reasons Peter Gabriel's 'Solsbury Hill' Is One of the Greatest Songs of All Time," *Billboard* (MRC Media, February 25, 2017), https://www.billboard.com/articles/columns/rock/7702117/peter-gabriel-solsbury-hill-anniversary-greatest-song.

In this case, being all from England, the *football team* would be what Americans would call a soccer team. In either case, though, to buy a *football team* is an extremely expensive affair. As if recognizing this, and perhaps abashed by their own conspicuous consumption, "Money" turns just as suddenly defensive, protective, and selfish:

> *Money, get back.*
>
> *I'm all right, Jack, keep your hands off my stack.*

This particular turn of phrase, *I'm all right, Jack*, has at least several decades of heritage. *I'm all right, Jack* is an old British phrase which indicates smug self-satisfaction to the point of rudeness. There is a somewhat cynical and bitter illustration of the phrase in the 1959 movie entitled, naturally, *I'm All Right, Jack*.

A satirical comedy of a very British sort, it is not known whether or not anyone in Pink Floyd actually saw the film. Members of the band would have been 13 to 16 years old when it came out, so it is certainly possible, inasmuch as it was very popular in England, winning the British Academy of Film and Television Arts (BAFTA) Best British Screenplay award. It also had a number of stars in its cast, including, among others, Ian Carmichael, Terry-Thomas, Peter Sellers (whose performance won him the BAFTA Best British Actor award), Richard Attenborough, Dennis Price, and even the pundit Malcolm Muggeridge.[171]

Interestingly, a clip from a Malcolm Muggeridge religious program on the BBC was featured in early — i.e., pre-Clare Torry — versions of "The Mortality Sequence," which eventually evolved into "The Great Gig in the Sky."[172]

The plot of *I'm All Right, Jack* is a tangle of labor versus management, with neither coming out the hero, a theme very much in keeping with "Money." As described by Glenn Erickson, who is the DVD Savant at www.dvdtalk.com, in a highly informative and witty review:[173]

> The insane setup is just credible enough to be offensive to all, as the script gleefully paints almost all Englishmen as silly fools corrupt beyond redemption. It stays safely neutral by lampooning businessmen as cads and charlatans, and the workingmen as lazy Communist sympathizers looking for unearned rewards, while opposing anything constructive.

---

[171] "Film in 1960," Film in 1960 | BAFTA Awards (British Academy of Film and Television Arts), accessed November 1, 2020, http://awards.bafta.org/award/1960/film.

[172] Kit Rae, "DARK SIDE OF THE MOON BOOTLEG SOUNDCLIPS and Other Stuff."

[173] Glenn Erickson, "The Peter Sellers Collection," DVD Savant Review: The Peter Sellers Collection (MH Sub I, LLC dba Internet Brands, March 3, 2003), http://www.dvdsavant.com/s744sell.html.

As in the facetious movie *I'm All Right Jack*, the song "Money" justifies its own defensiveness with a standoffish bit of everyone-is-doing-it, before returning to the plush embrace of lavishness:

> *Money, it's a hit.*
>
> *Don't give me that do goody good bullshit.*
>
> *I'm in the hi-fidelity first class traveling set,*
>
> *And I think I need a Lear jet.*

Taking Some Shine Off Glamor

Of course, the Learjet was *the* glamorous way to travel in the early 1970s, with Frank Sinatra and Elvis Presley establishing the gleaming new standard.[174] This glamour did not appeal to everyone, even if they happened to be a celebrity. Keith Richards of the Rolling Stones, for example, kept true to his roots in suggesting in the song "Happy" on the *Exile on Main St.* album that Learjets were not his preferred way to travel:

> *Never got a flash out of cocktails*
>
> *When I got some flesh off the bone*
>
> *Never got a lift out of Learjets*
>
> *When I can fly way back home.*[175]

It should be noted, in fairness to Learjet, however, that photographs which are said to depict a smiling Keith Richards on a Learjet flying from Los Angeles to San Diego in 1979 appear to be available.[176] This was several years after writing "Happy," so things may have changed in his view of this way of traveling.

In keeping with the love/hate relationship the world has with celebrity, the Learjet was sometimes viewed as the chariot of the self-absorbed. This can be heard vividly in the 1972 Carly Simon song, "You're So Vain:"

> *Well, I hear you went up to Saratoga,*
>
> *And your horse naturally won.*
>
> *Then you flew your Lear jet up to Nova Scotia,*
>
> *To see the total eclipse of the sun.*[177]

---

[174] "History of Private Jets, Planes & Aviation," Charter Jet One (Charter Jet One, June 2, 2020), https://charterjetone.com/history-of-private-jets-aviation/.

[175] Keith Richards and Mick Jagger, "Happy by The Rolling Stones," Songfacts (Sony/ATV Music Publishing LLC), accessed November 23, 2020, https://www.songfacts.com/lyrics/the-rolling-stones/happy.

[176] See, e.g., Henry Diltz, "Keith Richards and Ron Wood, Los Angeles, CA, 1979," (1979) (Morrison Hotel Gallery), accessed November 1, 2020, https://www.morrisonhotelgallery.com/photographs/cl9oZa/Keith-Richards-and-Ron-Wood-Los-Angeles-CA-1979.

[177] Carly Simon, "You're So Vain by Carly Simon," Songfacts (Universal Music Publishing Group), accessed November 23, 2020, https://www.songfacts.com/facts/carly-simon/

The presumably rich and famous erstwhile lover so bitterly mocked here could be the same person as the prickly focal character of "Money." But it could also be that very thing — the strident, sneering mockery of the singer — that evoked the defensiveness.

At first blush, it appears that another occurrence of synchronicity ties "You're So Vain" to *The Dark Side of the Moon*: Carly Simon's lover was flying to Nova Scotia to see a total eclipse of the sun. Her song was released only four months after an actual total eclipse visible in Nova Scotia on July 10, 1972.[178]

30. Shown here is the left front view of a Learjet, courtesy the Combined Military Service Digital Photographic Files, https://catalog.archives.gov.

As it actually happens, though, this coincidence seems to disappear, inasmuch as Simon indicated her song was actually written in 1971.[179] How she knew such details about the eclipse are not to be found, however. Some might think that she was referring to the total eclipse that could be seen in Nova Scotia on March 7, 1970,[180] but this does not make sense in light of the Saratoga Race Course schedule, which does not have racing in the Winter or Spring. So it remains an enigma of which eclipse she meant and how she knew to write about it.

---

youre-so-vain.

[178] S. P. Srivastava and R. A. Folinsbee, "Measurement of Variations in the Total Geomagnetic Field at Sea off Nova Scotia," *Canadian Journal of Earth Sciences* (Canadian Science Publishing, February 1, 1975), https://cdnsciencepub.com/doi/10.1139/e75-020.

[179] Daniel Kreps, "Carly Simon Refutes Theory That 'So Vain' Target Is David Geffen," *Rolling Stone* (Rolling Stone, LLC, a subsidiary of Penske Business Media, LLC, March 1, 2010), https://www.rollingstone.com/music/music-news/carly-simon-refutes-theory-that-so-vain-target-is-david-geffen-102891.

[180] "Map of Total Solar Eclipse on March 7, 1970," timeanddate.com (Time and Date AS), accessed November 1, 2020, https://www.timeanddate.com/eclipse/map/1970-march-7.

While luxury in the air for the literally high-flying lifestyle is appropriately associated with Learjet, the jet has also seen wide use in NASA and military functions. The glitzy side of the Learjet, though, seems emphasized by a bright, brassy, saxophone solo by Dick Parry, blaring after this verse.

When the saxophone solo has ended, a famously loud, anthemic, stadium-rock guitar solo bursts forth. After its crescendo, though, the guitar sound is boxed up somehow, for an interlude of almost intimate, contemplative picking. Of that stripped-down interlude, Gilmour said in an interview with *Guitar World* in February 1993, "It was my idea to break down and become dry and empty for the second chorus of the solo."[181]

After a few moments of this respite, the stadium-filling guitar and saxophone sound breaks out again. This extended saxophone/guitar instrumental set between verses lasts from about 2:02 to 5:10. Though the guitar solo is on many lists of bests and favorites, Gilmour himself is modest about his abilities. In an interview with Charlie Kendall of *The Source* on NBC Radio's Young Adult Network, Gilmour was downright humble:[182]

> I've never had fast fingers, they're really pretty slow compared to most, and the coordination between left and right hand and stuff is not great. If I start trying to do too fast then this one gets—the right one gets out of sync with the left hand, so I have to rely on other things. I rely on effects, fuzzboxes, anything that I can lay my hands on. Then I just try and make nice, sort of, melodies with it, like try to make it sing, I try to imagine that the guitar's kind of singing, you know?

The swift progression in "Money" from a person moderately satisfied with *a good job with more pay* to a caviar-eating reprobate weighing whether to buy a football team or a Learjet is not attributed to any accomplishment or merit. The abrupt transition may be because of some bit of luck, some striking it rich, but in any case it is not something that he has necessarily earned or deserves. Hearkening back to "Breathe" on Side One, the ambivalence about living the high life was already clear:

> For long you live and high you fly
>
> But only if you ride the tide
>
> And balanced on the biggest wave
>
> You race towards an early grave.

That is, "Breathe" embraces high flying, even though it is tied firmly to an early grave. The Side-Two person in "Money," in contrast, recognizes

[181] Alan di Perna, "David's Harp," in *Guitar World Presents Pink Floyd*, ed. Jeff Kitts and Brad Tolinski (Milwaukee, WI: Hal Leonard, 2002), p. 57.

[182] Charlie Kendall, "From the Source, with Host Charlie Kendall — Interview with David Gilmour," The Source (The Pink Floyd Fan Club, April 6, 1984), http://www.pink-floyd.org/artint/28.htm.

the inequality between rich and poor — more precisely, between rich and working class — but is not interested in equality if it is at the cost of any of his share:

> *Money it's a crime.*
>
> *Share it fairly but don't take a slice of my pie.*

He does not argue that he has earned or otherwise deserves his larger slice, or that there is any merit in covetousness, but justifies his refusal to give up any crumbs with the rationalization that everyone is doing it:

> *Money so they say*
>
> *Is the root of all evil today.*
>
> *But if you ask for a rise it's no surprise that they're*
>
> *Giving none away.*

As if to mirror the *Share it fairly but don't take a slice of my pie* ambivalence within the words of "Money," the spoken voices behind the lyrics return. At first, the voices seem united in their cause, whatever it is, clearly thinking that theirs was the moral high ground:

> *Huh, huh, I was in the right!*
>
> *Yes, absolutely in the right!*
>
> *I certainly was in the right!*[183]

The voices lose their unanimity quickly, however, and go back and forth, seeming at a loss for a real justification for whatever fight they were fighting:

> *Why does anyone do anything?*
>
> *I was definitely in the right. That geezer was cruising for a bruising.*
>
> *I don't know, I was really drunk at the time!*[184]

The last words of this exchange, entirely bereft of context from the snip-pets above, do not resolve anything, leaving things only that much more murky:

> *After he just told me he was in plugged in to number 2, he was asking why it wasn't coming up on fader eleven. So after yelling and screaming and telling him why it wasn't coming up on fader eleven, it came to a heavy blow, which sorted the matter out.*[185]

The music and chorus of "Money" are fading as these obscure clues to verbal or even physical altercations offstage are spoken. The ideas of struggle, whether internal or not, and how economics plays such a key role

---

[183] Kit Rae, "DARK SIDE OF THE MOON BOOTLEG SOUNDCLIPS and Other Stuff."
[184] *Id.*
[185] *Id.*

in the development of conflict, are elaborated further in the next song, "Us and Them," which is beginning even as "Money" is ending.

Track Eight: Us and Them

A slow, meditative organ begins "Us and Them" as the last sung *woo-woo-woo* of "Money" fades and one unidentified voice insists *I certainly was in the right!*

The pace of "Us and Them" is approximately as slow as that of "Breathe," and considerably more relaxed than that of "Money." It is interesting to hear "Us and Them" played together with "Breathe," layered over one another. The overlap seems merely coincidental, as opposed to planned or another bit of synchronicity — like any relation between *The Dark Side of the Moon* and *The Wizard of Oz*.

The organ volume begins to build in "Us and Them," and the unidentified voice tells us *I don't know, I was really drunk at the time!* At about the same time, another unidentified voice is heard briefly, shouting a lunatic *na-na-na-na*. This latter voice foreshadows "Brain Damage," but also somehow evokes "The Love Song of J. Alfred Prufrock" once again:

> I know the voices dying with a dying fall
>
> Beneath the music from a farther room.[186]

The organ is unaccompanied for more than 30 seconds in a calm, thoughtful way, relaxed and relaxing. After these cool moments, equally relaxed drums and guitar join in, soon followed by bass and then saxophone. It is not a rock sound, so much as a jazz combo in a smoky nightclub, sentimental. It is also a little melancholic, calling to mind "Lush Life," by Johnny Hartman and John Coltrane, or some other bluesy, moody song.

Just as in "Money," parts of the lyrics of "Us and Them" present a character speaking to someone whose responses we do not hear. The character's tone is mild, not harsh as it was in "Money." What is said, though, is blatantly self-serving, pious and sanctimonious:

> *Us, and them*
>
> *And after all we're only ordinary men.*
>
> *Me, and you.*
>
> *God only knows it's not what we would choose to do.*

This defensiveness and self-justification indicate that the speaker in "Us and Them" is not the same as the hero of "Breathe Reprise," who seemed at ease with himself. Further, although both are self-justifying, the character of

---

[186] T. S. Eliot, "Prufrock and Other Observations."

the defensiveness in "Us and Them" is also different from that of the narrator of "Money." In "Money," the singer explicitly recognized and acknowledged the inequities that he exploited and enjoyed. In "Us and Them," in contrast, the singer is trying to count himself out of those who brought or supported whatever conflict is at issue.

Inasmuch as we never hear an affirmation or denial following these initial proclamations of "Us and Them," we do not know if the person being addressed is in accord, or whether there is even any collective "we" to be referred to at all. Moreover, in these first few lines, much like in the extra voice additions at the bridge between "Money" and "Us and Them," the nature of the conflict being discussed remains ambiguous.

"Us and Them" is haunted by the possibility that these sentiments could arise amidst some dispute on a smaller scale. It could be that these words are being uttered after some business corner-cutting, some secret betrayal in an intimate relationship, spoken a safe distance from a burning building with unrescued people inside, or at the gravesite of a person who would have lived with one of the kidneys of one of the ostensible mourners. Hypocrisy wears many coats.

But the dominant theme of war arises quickly in "Us and Them," with the next lines being unambiguously war-related:

Forward, he cried from the rear,

and the front rank died.

And the general sat and the lines on the map

moved from side to side.

The speaker of these four lines does not seem to be the same as the one in the first four lines, insisting on his ordinariness. The initial speaker is keen to distinguish himself from the generals, the ones prosecuting war. But the insincere tone of the first lines nonetheless suggests tacit complicity between the first speaker and the second.

As it happens, moreover, such tacit complicity is much more the rule than the exception — that is, ordinariness is not necessarily a good thing at all. With respect to war, the darker side of blending in and doing what everyone else was doing has been amply demonstrated.

For example, shortly before the release of *The Dark Side of the Moon*, during the 1972 Presidential election campaign, the candidate George McGovern was explicitly and emphatically anti-war, calling for an immediate end to the Vietnam War. Richard Nixon, in contrast, labeled opposition to the war as Leftist extremism. Nixon won handily, with McGovern winning only Massachusetts and the District of Columbia.[187]

Nixon's mandate was a remarkably broad swath of ordinary men, as opposed to merely any stereotype of Republicans. An internal memorandum from the Nixon campaign cited the results of a survey taken by CBS on election day, indicating that Nixon had secured 56% of the Catholic vote, 57% of Blue Collar Workers, and 48% of the 18–24 year olds voting. Nixon even won 37% of registered Democrats.[188] These were all groups that typically supported the Democratic candidate, but did not in 1972.

No one who voted for Nixon would likely have claimed out loud to have wanted the Vietnam War to continue, but the landslide vote was nonetheless manifestly against a candidate whose main campaign platform was ending the war. This allowed Nixon to continue the war, bolstered by his landslide mandate from ordinary men.

It is also important to underscore that this support of Nixon was not just among older, established voters. This was the first election in which the voice of youthful voters was heard, but, as indicated above, 48% of this youth vote went to Nixon. That is, among the very people buying *The Dark Side of the Moon*, about half voted for Richard Nixon.

The activist image of Flower Children and the Woodstock Generation is thus only half the story, quite literally. This is not a comfortable image. Some might argue about Nixon as the superior candidate in the then-existing economy and so on. This debate will not be pursued here, other than to comment that dying in a war is not the same as being out of work.

In other ways, however, what ordinary men are capable of had been made disturbingly clear.

Another stark illustration came from an infamous set of experiments conducted in the early Sixties by the Yale University psychologist Stanley Milgram. In these experiments, Milgram had set out to find some practical information about the extent to which people — ordinary people —

---

[187] David S. Broder, "Nixon Wins Landslide Victory; Democrats Hold Senate, House McGovern Admits Defeat; President Calls for Harmony," *The Washington Post* (WP Company, November 8, 1972), p. A01, www.washingtonpost.com/wp-srv/national/long-term/watergate/articles/110872-1.htm.

[188] R. M. Teeter, "Memo; R. M. Teeter to H. R. Haldeman; Undated, but Ca. November 8, 1972; Folder 40-05-H.R. Haldeman; Box 40; Folder 5; Contested Materials Collection," Richard Nixon Presidential Library (National Archives, November 1972), https://www.nixonlibrary.gov/sites/default/files/virtuallibrary/documents/contested/contested_box_40/Contested-40-05.pdf, p. 24.

responded to authority when that authority was telling them to do things that ran counter to their supposed moral values.[189]

The experiment, which has become well known, and even the subject of a quietly disturbing Peter Gabriel song, "We Do What We're Told (Milgram's 37)," involved groups of three people — nominally a researcher, a teacher, and a learner. The teachers were volunteers who had responded to an advertisement claiming to need people to participate in a study of learning. These volunteers were paid a token $4.00 for an hour of their time, according to the advertisement for the project, and were told by the researchers that they would be assisting specifically in a study of how punishment affected memory and learning.[190] This is what the volunteers presumably believed.

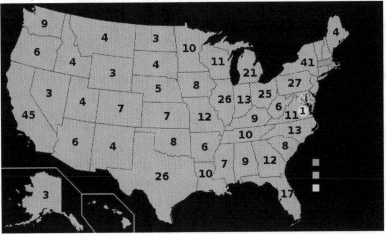

31. This map of the 1972 Electoral College, which has been released to public domain, was created and uploaded by Steve Sims in August 2008, and may be found in its latest version at https://commons.wikimedia.org.

The teacher would read lists of word pairs to the learner, who was strapped into what looked a lot like an electric chair, with what appeared to be electrodes attached to his arms. Specifically, the teacher read the first word of a pair, followed by four words for the learner to choose from. If the learner chose correctly, they would move to the next pair. If the learner did not choose correctly, however, the teacher was instructed to deliver an electric shock to the learner. The shocks increased by an apparent 15 volts for

[189] McLeod, S. A. (2017, February 05). The Milgram Shock Experiment. Simply Psychology. https://www.simplypsychology.org/milgram.html.

[190] Gregorio Billikopf Encina, Milgram's Experiment on Obedience to Authority (The Regents of the University of California, November 15, 2004), https://nature.berkeley.edu/ucce50/ag-labor/7article/article35.htm.

each incorrect answer, with a maximum voltage of 450 volts. At least that was what the teachers were told.

In fact, and unbeknownst to the volunteers, the learners were actors, and the shocks were taped sounds. As the fictitious voltage increased, the learners would protest more and more loudly, then yell, scream, and even bang against the wall separating them from the teachers. In the event the teachers were reluctant to go forward with the testing because of these apparent reactions, the researcher would give them verbal prods to prompt them to continue.

Though they may have initially complained and delayed, *all* of the volunteers continued the experiment to what they thought was 300 volts, while fully 65% of the volunteers went to the highest level, 450 volts. It is worth repeating: *All of the volunteers* gave the learners what they thought was a 300 volt shock.

Reflecting on these results in an article he wrote in 1974, "The Perils of Obedience," Milgram observed that how people on the whole behave is not terribly well correlated to ideas of obedience found in philosophy or the law. Even as the victims were crying out, ordinary people bowed to authority. The main finding of his experiment, and the main feature demanding further study, was the appalling level to which people submitted to command.[191]

Milgram's results were widely questioned and challenged,[192] but substantial reproductions of and variations on Milgram's experiment showed that in every iteration, a sizeable portion of the volunteers would inflict what they thought was the maximum shock.[193]

Other experiments included the equally infamous 1971 Stanford experiment in which volunteers were paid $15 a day to act as prisoners or guards in what they knew was a psychological experiment.[194] As with the Milgram experiment, the volunteers were responding to an advertisement, and in this case were screened to make sure that they did not have criminal back-

---

[191] Cited by Saul McLeod, The Milgram Shock Experiment. A copy of "The Perils of Obedience" from *Harper's Magazine* 247, no. 1483, December 1973, may be found at https://is.muni.cz/el/1423/podzim2013/PSY268/um/43422262/Milgram_-_perils_of_obediance.pdf, hosted by the Faculty of Informatics, Masaryk University, Brno, Czech Republic.

[192] Cari Romm, "Rethinking One of Psychology's Most Infamous Experiments," *The Atlantic* (Atlantic Media Company, January 28, 2015), https://www.theatlantic.com/health/archive/2015/01/rethinking-one-of-psychologys-most-infamous-experiments/384913/.

[193] *See, e.g.*, Robin Andrews, "Scientists Just Replicated The Infamous Milgram Experiment," IFLScience (IFLScience, March 17, 2017), https://www.iflscience.com/brain/scientists-replicated-infamous-milgram-experiment.

[194] Philip G Zimbardo, "2. Setting Up," Stanford Prison Experiment (Social Psychology Network, 1999), https://www.prisonexp.org/setting-up.

grounds, psychological problems, and the like, and split into two groups —
prisoners and guards — by a literal coin-flip.[195]

The researchers had constructed a prison mock-up in the basement of
the Stanford Psychology Building, which included boarded-up windows,
numbered doors with steel bars, a closet set aside for solitary confinement,
and video surveillance and bugging of the cells.[196] The researchers applied a
variety of steps to half of the volunteers to mimic the intake of actual prisoners, while the other half were given minimal training — little beyond being
told that they should do what they thought necessary to maintain order and
command respect.[197]

32. This advertisement for the now-famous experiment by Prof. Stanley
Milgram of the Yale Psychology Department, ran in the *New Haven Register* on
June 18, 1961. Uploaded by Olivier Hammam, it is on commons.wikimedia.
org.

The granular details of the disturbingly rapid development and/or decay
of each set of volunteers is both fascinating and deeply troubling, with even
the parents of the volunteers falling into line with their designated roles,

---

[195] *Id.*

[196] *Id.*

[197] Philip G Zimbardo, Stanford Prison Experiment, https://www.prisonexp.org/arrival,
https://www.prisonexp.org/guards.

and bearing out vividly why the experiment was halted half-way through the two weeks initially planned.[198] The highly detailed website that Philip Zimbardo has set up, www.prisonexp.org, provides this granularity, as well as insight into the myriad questions raised by the behavior of both sets of volunteers.

The Milgram experiment and the Stanford experiment both made efforts to be reflective of normal society; as such, they support a dim view of human conduct. The protestation in "Us and Them," *after all we're only ordinary men*, thus presents an irony, insofar as ordinary men routinely choose to do ghastly things whenever they are told or allowed to.

One would like to think, given the nervousness shown by the Milgram subjects, that without scientists, generals, or other authorities exhorting them to their evils, that people are on the whole good. But nervousness or reluctance is not the same as resistance. As Milgram had phrased it in his 1963 report:[199]

> At one point, [the participant] pushed his fist into his forehead and muttered: "Oh God, let's stop it." And yet he continued to respond to every word of the experiment and obeyed to the end.

No Shortage of Authorities

Unfortunately, there has never been a shortage of take-charge types with clip boards or batons to tell others what to do, relying on the submission of those whom they attempt to direct. As Arthur Koestler, nominated three times for the Nobel Prize, had observed in *The Ghost in the Machine*:[200]

> The lessons of the past have been wasted; history not only repeats itself, it seems to be laboring under a neurotic compulsion to do so.

As if recognizing this power of telling people what to do, the "Us and Them" vocals become like the shouting of someone giving orders on these words:

> *Forward, he cried from the rear,*
>
> *and the front rank died.*

This shouted lead is accompanied by a female chorus, complementing the violence of words with a wordless lament. The chorus falls silent when the song returns to the quieter verses.

---

[198] Id,, https://www.prisonexp.org/grievances.

[199] Stanley Milgram, "Behavioral Study of Obedience," Journal of Abnormal and Social Psychology 67 (1963): pp. 317-78, cited in Daniel M. Wegner and Kurt Gray, *The Mind Club Who Thinks, What Feels, and Why It Matters* (New York, NY: Penguin Random House, 2016), p. 304.

[200] A. Koestler, *The Ghost in the Machine*, pp. 325-26.

The days of captains with sabers drawn leading their troops into battle are gone, though the ground troops fighting has lasted. "Us and Them" reminds us that the higher the rank, the farther from the actual fighting the individual will be (*Forward, he cried from the rear*), and that it is the troops on the ground that make up the majority military casualties (*and the front rank died*).

33. World War I German shock troops rising from trenches to attack, 1917 — 1918. This photograph is courtesy the German Federal Archives, Bundesarchiv, Bild 146-1974-132-26A / Unknown / CC-BY-SA 3.0, and is available on commons.wikimedia.org through a cooperation project.

And the general sat and the lines on the map

moved from side to side.

Of course, the idea that war is orchestrated by men who are not themselves in danger is a common theme in literature and poetry, as is the idea of so many battles being for them — the generals — an abstract exercise in geometry. As absurd as it may sound, battle lines moving from side to side was not something invented or exaggerated at all. In trench warfare, every literal foot of land was bitterly contested, and a piece of land might be gained, lost, and gained again and again, at great cost in soldiers' lives. For example, in his moving autobiographical story of World War I, *Goodbye to All That*, Robert Graves describes exactly that:[201]

> The remaining territorial battalion joined the First Division in France early in 1915, and quite un-necessarily lost its machine-guns at Givenchy. Regimental machine-guns, in 1915, were regarded almost as sacred. To lose them before the wiping-out of the entire battalion was considered as shameful as losing the regimental colours would have been in any eighteenth- or nineteenth-century battle. The terri-

---

[201] Robert Graves, *Goodbye to All That* (London: Folio Society, 1981), pp. 76-77.

torial machine-gun officer who abandoned his guns had congratulated himself on removing the bolts; this would make them useless to the enemy. But he had forgotten the boxes of spare-parts. The Second Battalion made a raid in the same sector, a year and a half later, and recaptured one of the guns, which had been busy against our trenches ever since.

Though the tone of Graves' description is breezy in a very British stiff-upper-lip sort of way, it should not obscure the fact that the First Division had moved up as far as Givenchy, were driven back, and took a year and a half of fighting to re-take the exact same position. Such was the image-consciousness of these soldiers, moreover, that the initial loss of the regiment's machine guns before the battalion was slaughtered was seen as something shameful. This disproportionate image-consciousness is consistent with the compliance of the Milgram subjects, who do not wish to be seen as disobedient when told to move up the voltage.

Graves' anecdote of the machine-gun officer's removal of bolts is on par with any of the fictional absurdities of Joseph Heller's classic *Catch-22*. But the sharpness of "Us and Them" contrasts with the low-key tone of *Goodbye to All That* or the more overt humor and satire of *Catch-22*. "Us and Them" is much closer in tone to the bitterness of the 1963 song, "Masters of War," written by the winner of the 2016 Nobel Prize for Literature, Bob Dylan.

Though both "Us and Them" and "Masters of War" were written during the Vietnam War, the breadth of these songs is much greater. In the case of "Us and Them," the issues raised in the song were not at all abstract to the members of Pink Floyd. World War II was still going on when three of the members of them were born: Richard Wright was born July 28, 1943; Roger Waters, September 6, 1943; Nick Mason, January 27, 1944. The war was less than a year over when the fourth, David Gilmour, was born, on March 6, 1946.[202] Victory in Europe (VE) Day was first celebrated on May 8, 1945; Victory in Japan (VJ) Day was first celebrated in the United Kingdom August 15, 1945.[203]

The destruction to Britain was severe, and obvious vestiges of the war persisted for a long time in the United Kingdom. During the Blitz, as described in the *British Official Histories History of the Second World War*, "Some 40,000 British civilians had been killed, another 46,000 injured, and more

[202] Jeremy Brown, "Newsweek Special Edition: The Artists Behind Pink Floyd's Sound," *Newsweek* (Newsweek Digital LLC, June 8, 2015), https://www.newsweek.com/pink-floyd-sound-353897.

[203] History.com Editors, "V-J Day," History.com (A&E Television Networks, October 14, 2009), https://www.history.com/topics/world-war-ii/v-j-day.

than a million houses damaged."[204] With such widespread destruction, no one in the UK at the time was without a first-person story. The young people who would become the members of Pink Floyd would certainly have heard some of them.

This fact is not always really comprehended by people in the United States, as, with the important exception of Pearl Harbor, the U.S. homeland had not suffered any attack. At least one reviewer of the movie *I'm All Right, Jack*, described in the "Money" chapter, felt it was the portrayal of this persistence of war effects that made the film a stretch for American audiences.[205] As will be shown, the reality of widespread misery comes into play again in the last verses of the song.

As was the case in the first verse, when the second verse of "Us and Them" begins, it is not unambiguously about war. It could be about any dispute in which two sides feel strongly enough about the rightness of their cause to continue to fight, but which to an outsider does not seem worth the effort:

Black and blue

And who knows which is which and who is who.

Up and down.

But in the end it's only round and round.

Underscoring the ambiguity about what the conflict in question may be, as these lines are sung the music returns to the intimate, nightclub sound, contrasting with the thundering sound of the end of the last verse. There is even an insouciant flourish of the piano at *Up*, adding a cheerful bit of buoyancy. The ping right after the phrase *Just a little pinprick* in the song "Comfortably Numb" years later, from their album *The Wall*, seems a throwback to that "Us and Them" flourish.

Again, at this specific point in "Us and Them," it is hard to say what dispute — or even what kind of dispute — is being addressed. This evokes the same situational ambiguity as accompanied the beginning of the song. Moreover, the contrasts chosen — *Black/blue, Up/down* — suggest that to an outsider the differences between the sides may not be as clear nor as significant as they may seem to the participants.

The generality of lines is also borne out by the avoidance of contrasts that would trigger obvious then-current conflicts. The first line of this

---

[204] Denis Richards, "The Blitz," in *HyperWar: Royal Air Force 1939—1945: Volume I: The Fight at Odds* [Chapter VII] (HyperWar Foundation), accessed November 20, 2020, http://www.ibiblio.org/hyperwar/UN/UK/UK-RAF-I/UK-RAF-I-7.html.

[205] Mark Bourne, "The DVD Journal: Quick Reviews: I'm All Right Jack," *The DVD Journal* | Quick Reviews: I'm All Right Jack (The DVD Journal), accessed November 20, 2020, http://www.dvdjournal.com/quickreviews/i/imallrightjack.q.shtml.

verse opposes *Black* and *blue* — as opposed to black and white, with their racial overtones, or orange and green, with their implication of the situation in Northern Ireland. This is in very stark contrast to Paul McCartney and Wings' first single, "Give Ireland Back to the Irish," relating directly to the Bloody Sunday massacre on January 30, 1972, which was banned from broadcast by the BBC[206].

As in *Black* and *blue*, the second opposition in "Us and Them," of *Up* and *down*, does not point to any familiar dispute. In contrast, there might have been some suggestion of socioeconomic disparity were "top" and "bottom" opposed. Certainly "left" and "right" would have had political overtones. Hence, the pairs chosen kept the listener from restricting the scope of conflicts "Us and Them" might apply to.

This innocuousness is short lived, however. As the next verse begins, the music becomes loud again, the chorus again keens, and the next lines revert to an unambiguously military context, with both military recruiters and protestors accosting people on the street:

> *Haven't you heard it's a battle of words*
>
> *The poster bearer cried.*
>
> *Listen son, said the man with the gun*
>
> *There's room for you inside.*

That people are out on the streets to hear these admonitions and invitations may suggest that they are not otherwise occupied at work, an idea elaborated on further in later verses.

While the dynamic of the poster-bearing anti-war protestor versus armed Army recruiters seemed a commonplace in the Vietnam era, the virulence of "Us and Them" may instead have had its roots in opposition to World War II. While there was much widespread devastation in the UK, as discussed above, the run-up to World War II and the carnage it wrought had particularly personal focus for, and shaped so much of the outlook of, Roger Waters, who wrote the lyrics to "Us and Them."

Early in World War II, Waters' father was a conscientious objector who drove an ambulance during the Blitz. Waters' father changed his mind about his conscientious objector status, however, and joined the Territorial Army in September, 1943. He was killed only five months later, in February, 1944, when Waters was only five months old.[207]

[206] Stephen Dowling, "Banned: The Songs Deemed 'Too Dangerous' for the BBC," BBC Culture (BBC, June 20, 2019), http://www.bbc.com/culture/story/20190620-banned-the-songs-deemed-too-dangerous-for-the-bbc.

[207] Nick Squires, "Roger Waters Memorialises His Fallen WWII Father," *The Telegraph* (Telegraph Media Group, February 18, 2014), https://www.telegraph.co.uk/news/world-

It is interesting to consider what factors made Water's father change his mind about his conscientious objector status — whether it was the efforts of recruiters and their posters and slogans. Whatever the factors may have been, Waters' own profound bitterness over the loss of his father can be heard here in "Us and Them," and would become the autobiographical foundation of *The Wall* a few years later.

As if to give a bit of breathing space after this intense verse, there is a break in the singing, with a flowing instrumental interlude with a bouncy bit of piano, accompanied by another of the spoken parts:[208]

> *I mean, they're gonna kill ya, so if you give 'em a quick short, sharp, shock, they won't do it again. Dig it? I mean he got off lightly, 'cause I would've given him a thrashing, I only hit him once. It was only a difference of opinion, but really, I mean good manners don't cost nothing do they, eh?*

This voice, speaking of a brief but lively personal altercation, brings back the ambiguity of parts of the song, keeping it from being simply and solely about war on a world scale.

34. Protest against the Vietnam War in front of the Justice Department in Washington, D.C., on April 24, 1971. Photograph by Warren K. Leffler, 1971. https://www.loc.gov/item/2017646299/.

As was the case with the phrase *I'm all right, Jack* in "Money," the phrase *short, sharp, shock* in "Us and Them" has a very deep history. Its first appearance seems to have been in a translation of the ancient Roman poet Horace,

news/europe/italy/10646870/Roger-Waters-memorialises-his-fallen-WWII-father.html.
[208] Kit Rae, "DARK SIDE OF THE MOON BOOTLEG SOUNDCLIPS and Other Stuff."

who wrote, among other things, social satires. In his *Satire I*, as translated by the Corpus Professor of Latin at the University of Oxford, John Conington, in 1870, Horace shares how even in the year 35 B.C.[209] people thought the grass was always greener on the other side of the fence:

> How comes it, say, Maecenas, if you can,
>
> That none will live like a contented man
>
> Where choice or chance directs, but each must praise
>
> The folk who pass through life by other ways?
>
> "Those lucky merchants!" cries the soldier stout,
>
> When years of toil have well-nigh worn him out:
>
> What says the merchant, tossing o'er the brine?
>
> "Yon soldier's lot is happier, sure, than mine:
>
> One short, sharp shock, and presto! all is done:
>
> Death in an instant comes, or victory's won."
>
> The lawyer lauds the farmer, when a knock
>
> Disturbs his sleep at crowing of the cock:
>
> The farmer, dragged to town on business, swears
>
> That only citizens are free from cares.[210]

Thus, for Horace, the *short, sharp, shock* was the quick death of the soldier, of which the shopkeeper was jealous. This deep heritage is ironic in "Us and Them," a song decrying soldier deaths.

The *short, sharp, shock* phrase was revived and popularized in 1885 by W. S. Gilbert and Arthur Sullivan in their famous comic opera, *The Mikado*. There is no clear indication that Gilbert or Sullivan were intentionally echoing Horace. It must be said, however, that they were certainly well read. From their opera *Ruddigore; or, The Witch's Curse* (or, as much more colorfully expressed in the 1887 printed libretto, *An Entirely Original Supernatural Opera, | in two acts, | entitled | Ruddigore; | or, | The Witch's Curse!*) it may be inferred that such reading included Horace, however:

> As a poet, I'm tender and quaint —
>
> I've passion and fervour and grace —

---

[209] Michael Grant, "Horace," *Encyclopædia Britannica* (Encyclopædia Britannica, Inc.), accessed November 20, 2020, https://www.britannica.com/biography/Horace-Roman-poet.

[210] Horace, *The Satires, Epistles, and Art of Poetry of Horace*, trans. John Conington (London: Bell and Daldy, 1870), p. 1. Available online as Horace, "The Satires, Epistles, and Art of Poetry of Horace, Tr. into Engl. Verse by ... Quintus Horatius Flaccus," trans. John Conington, Internet Archive (Oxford University, January 3, 2010), https://archive.org/details/satire-sepistles00flacgoog.

From Ovid and Horace To Swinburne and Morris,

They all of them take a back place.[211]

The plot of *The Mikado* is indeed silly, satirizing British politics of the day.[212] In the first act, three officials and nobles have been informed in a letter from the Emperor of Japan, the Mikado, that there must be an execution in their town, or it will be humiliatingly reduced to the rank of a village — another example of disproportionate image-consciousness discussed in the context of "Us and Them." The three worthies discuss among themselves who ought to be beheaded, concluding with this contemplation thereof:

To sit in solemn silence in a dull, dark dock,

In a pestilential prison, with a lifelong lock,

Awaiting the sensation of a short, sharp shock,

From a cheap and chippy chopper on a big black block![213]

That is, once again, the *short, sharp, shock* as performed in *The Mikado*, is fatal. And so, even though the voices heard in "Us and Them" seem to be describing a minor personal fracas, the phrasing they use nonetheless evokes a heritage of a much more serious conflict.

An extended saxophone solo begins a more relaxed interlude. It then turns raucous, however, accompanied by the wailing chorus. This reaches a crescendo, and then falls again. When the lyrics resume to the cooled tempo, it is a quiet, resigned contemplation of widespread poverty:

It can't be helped but there's a lot of it about.

With, without.

And who'll deny it's what the fighting's all about?

The phrase *Down and out* may be a reference to George Orwell's *Down and Out in Paris and London*, published in 1933. While much better known for his dystopian novel *1984*, Orwell's gritty, detailed descriptions of the sordid,

[211] William Schwenck Gilbert and Arthur Sullivan, "An Entirely Original Supernatural Opera, | in two acts, | entitled | Ruddigore; | or, | The Witch's Curse!: Sullivan, Arthur, 1842–1900, Composer; Gilbert, William Schwenck, 1836–1911, Librettist," Internet Archive (London: Chappell, publisher, January 22, 1887; Harold B. Lee Library, Brigham Young University, Digitizing sponsor, May 13, 2013), https://archive.org/details/entirely-original1887sull.

[212] Chorus America, "The Mikado, The Collegiate Chorale, Carnegie Hall," The Mikado | Chorus America (Chorus America, April 2012), https://www.chorusamerica.org/calendar/mikado.

[213] William Schwenck Gilbert and Arthur Sullivan, Full text of "The Mikado Or The Town Of Titipu" (Universal Digital Library, July 1, 2004), https://archive.org/stream/mikadoorthetowno002227mbp/mikadoorthetowno002227mbp_djvu.txt.

squalid conditions of life in Winston Smith's world of *1984* were doubtless informed by the weeks and months Orwell lived as an actual tramp and recorded the experience in *Down and Out*.

35. Poster for a Federal Music Project production of *The Mikado* at the Philharmonic Auditorium, from the Works Projects Administration Poster Collection, courtesy the Library of Congress. Sullivan, Arthur, Mikado, and U.S. Federal Music Project. https://www.loc.gov/item/98517745/*Down and out*

The offhandedness of *It can't be helped but there's a lot of it about* in "Us and Them" seems very in keeping with much of the minimal sentimentality in *Down and Out in Paris and London:*[214]

For, when you are approaching poverty, you make one discovery which outweighs some of the others. You discover boredom and mean

---

[214] George Orwell, Full text of "Down And Out In Paris And London — English — George Orwell" (The University of Adelaide Library, May 14, 2004), https://archive.org/stream/DownAndOutInParisAndLondon-English-GeorgeOrwell/orwellparislondon_djvu.txt., Chapter III.

complications and the beginnings of hunger, but you also discover the great redeeming feature of poverty: the fact that it annihilates the future. Within certain limits, it is actually true that the less money you have, the less you worry. When you have a hundred francs in the world you are liable to the most craven panics. When you have only three francs you are quite indifferent; for three francs will feed you till tomorrow, and you cannot think further than that. You are bored, but you are not afraid. You think vaguely, 'I shall be starving in a day or two — shocking, isn't it?' And then the mind wanders to other topics. A bread and margarine diet does, to some extent, provide its own anodyne.

In the context of this excerpt, it hard to tell whether Orwell is using *anodyne* in the sense of being a pain-killer or just something inoffensive. It may be both: Orwell does not seem to be suffering from hunger, exactly, but only bored, and the other topics his mind wanders to do not seem upsetting.

After its resigned contemplation of widespread poverty, "Us and Them" once again becomes harsh, and the chorus again joins in. Despite the chorus, this verse does not refer to war, but to a more disdainful view of the poor:

Out of the way, it's a busy day

I've got things on my mind.

These two lines seem the voice of a disdainful businessman, impatient with anyone without the wherewithal to hold down a job, brushing past the beggars on the street, who may well be homeless veterans.[215] Such an attitude is as familiar today as it was to Orwell in 1933:[216]

It is worth saying something about the social position of beggars, for when one has consorted with them, and found that they are ordinary human beings, one cannot help being struck by the curious attitude that society takes towards them. People seem to feel that there is some essential difference between beggars and ordinary 'working' men. They are a race apart — outcasts, like criminals and prostitutes. Working men 'work', beggars do not 'work'; they are parasites, worthless in their very nature. It is taken for granted that a beggar does not 'earn' his living, as a bricklayer or a literary critic 'earns' his. He is a mere social excrescence, tolerated because we live in a humane age, but essentially despicable.

Finally, the last two lines of "Us and Them," *For the want of the price of tea and a slice/The old man died*, hearkens back to *Down and Out in Paris and London*

---

[215] Leo Shane III, "Number of Homeless Vets Rises for First Time in Seven Years," *Military Times* (Sightline Media Group, December 6, 2017), https://www.militarytimes.com/veterans/2017/12/06/number-of-homeless-veterans-nationwide-rises-for-first-time-in-seven-years.

[216] George Orwell, *Down And Out In Paris And London*, Chapter XXXI.

very closely. After a night in a London lodging-house that cost him a shilling, Orwell went to a coffee shop, where the following colloquy took place:[217]

'Could I have some tea and bread and butter?' I said to the girl.

She stared. 'No butter, only marg,' she said, surprised. And she repeated the order in the phrase that is to London what the eternal *coup de rouge*[218] is to Paris: 'Large tea and two slices!'

On the wall beside my pew there was a notice saying 'Pocketing the sugar not allowed,' and beneath it some poetic customer had written:

He that takes away the sugar,

Shall be called a dirty —

but someone else had been at pains to scratch out the last word. This was England. The tea-and-two-slices cost threepence halfpenny, leaving me with eight and twopence.

With the words *The old man died*, "Us and Them" abruptly breaks off and the instrumental "Any Colour You Like" begins without losing a beat.

Track Nine: Any Colour You Like

Synthesizers and guitars with copious effects dominate the instrumental "Any Colour You Like." The song is a catchy dialogue between synthesizer and guitar, in which it is sometimes difficult to tell which instrument is being heard. About 1:20 into the song, however, there is a jarring, heavily-effected guitar, reminiscent of the synthesizer chords at about 0:57 into "One Of These Days" or the guitar chords at about 10:01 into "Echoes," both off their 1971 release, *Meddle*. It also faintly recalls the lunatic *na-na-na-na* between "Money" and "Us and Them."

Because there are no lyrics to "Any Colour You Like," nor any voice-over comments, it is of course open to speculation as to what it is "about," to the extent that a song has intellectual or narrative meaning outside of its social or programmatic context. There is some scat vocalization by David Gilmour, but that, too, is not amenable to interpretation.

One explanation given by Roger Waters, however, related the title back to the patter of people selling miscellaneous things out of the backs of vans on the streets of Cambridge. An assortment of cups and plates for sale might be accompanied by the sales pitch, "Any colour you like, they're all blue." Waters has interpreted this as the appearance of a choice where there is none.[219]

---

[217] George Orwell, *Down And Out In Paris And London*, Chapter XXIV.
[218] Glass of red wine.
[219] Kit Rae, "DARK SIDE OF THE MOON BOOTLEG SOUNDCLIPS and Other Stuff."

36. Henry Ford's 1908 4-cylinder Model T, in any color so long as it's black. Photograph taken by the Grogan Photo Co., Danville, Ill., courtesy the Library of Congress. https://www.loc.gov/item/97512745/.

This explanation recalls the dilemma posed by Hobson's Choice, a concept going back centuries. Hobson, it was said, rented out horses in Cambridge, of all places. Customers were told that they got the horse nearest the door. If they didn't like that selection, their only alternative was to leave empty-handed.[220]

This explanation seems fittingly glib for the funky, upbeat feel of the song, given its placement between the much more serious songs "Us and Them" and "Brain Damage." As abruptly as it started, "Any Colour You Like" ends and "Brain Damage" begins, with no pause or bridge at all between them.

Track Ten: Brain Damage

"Brain Damage" is a slower song, sung by Roger Waters, similar in both respects to the song "If" from the 1970 album *Atom Heart Mother*. Like "Brain

---

[220] Gary Martin, "'Hobson's Choice' — the Meaning and Origin of This Phrase," Phrasefinder, accessed November 20, 2020, https://www.phrases.org.uk/meanings/hobsons-choice.html.

Damage," the older song "If" refers very directly to mental illness and treatment, and also ties the speaker's behavior metaphorically to the moon:

If I were to sleep, I could dream

If I were afraid, I could hide

If I go insane, please don't put your wires in my brain

If I were the moon, I'd be cool

If I were a rule, I would bend

If I were a good man, I'd understand the spaces between friends

If I were alone, I would cry

And if I were with you, I'd be home and dry

And if I go insane, will you still let me join in with the game?

The guitar at the beginning of "Brain Damage" has a distinctly bell-like quality, calling to mind *The tolling of the iron bell* from "Breathe Reprise." In "Brain Damage," however, it is not faith that brings one to their knees. The drum line of "Brain Damage" also recalls another song, "Speak to Me," with its distinct heartbeat sound. Perhaps this musical motif is to call up the chaos that seemed to inform "Speak to Me."

The lyrics of "Brain Damage" start with a repeated line that for Pink Floyd fans has two meanings. Also, beneath these lines, there is a barely heard chuckle that reinforces the double entendre:

The lunatic is on the grass.

The lunatic is on the grass.

Of course, grass is a common nickname for marijuana. And, also of course, from their very first performances, Pink Floyd has been associated with drug use.[221] While the band generally discounted its involvement in drugs, their temperate position was not bolstered by songs like "Alan's Psychedelic Breakfast" on *Atom Heart Mother*, for example. Accordingly, to hear Pink Floyd sing that *The lunatic is on the grass* is to immediately assume that this is a song about marijuana use.

Across the ocean, drugs were also in widespread use and often associated closely with particular bands. Light shows that became the foundation for the spectacular effects that accompany so many shows today were also growing in popularity. At least one band in the United States brought the two together, the Velvet Underground, as a part of Andy Warhol's Exploding Plastic Inevitable shows.

---

[221]https://www.rollingstone.com/music/features/the-madness-majesty-of-pink-floyd-20070405.

37. Marijuana, often called grass, was frequently associated with psychedelic music. This photograph of a cannabis leaf is courtesy Dohduhdah via Wikimedia Commons.

As described on the Alden Projects gallery website for their *Warhol and the Velvet Underground: Intermedia Collaborations 1966–67* exhibition, the Velvet Underground experience included unconventional combinations of music, film, dance, and light shows, to make them more than just a band on a stage.[222] In terms of drugs, moreover, the Velvet Underground was very direct, with songs like "I'm Waiting for the Man," about trying to obtain heroin, and "Heroin," vividly describing the effects of the drug and its almost irresistible draw.

In its own way, "Brain Damage" is as serious in implication as "Heroin." "Brain Damage" is about much more than drugs and their effects, however, as discussed below.

Notwithstanding the level of their audience's use over the years, the drug use of the active members of Pink Floyd at the time of recording *The Dark Side of the Moon* was rather modest. How modest depends on which partic-

---

[222] Todd Alden, "Warhol and the Velvet Underground: Intermedia Collaborations 1966-67," 2014, http://www.aldenprojects.com/2014/11/warhol-and-velvet-underground.html.

ular account you read. Note the expression, as well as the words, of David Gilmour when he is asked about drugs in an interview in the 1972 movie, *Pink Floyd: Live at Pompeii*.

The drug use of Syd Barrett, one of the founders of the band who did not actually play on *The Dark Side of the Moon*, was apparently not at all modest. His subsequent behavioral descent influenced much of Pink Floyd's work after he was excluded from the band, including the song "Brain Damage." The next few lines of "Brain Damage" begin to make very clear that mental illness, as opposed to marijuana, is to be considered:

Remembering games and daisy chains and laughs.

Got to keep the loonies on the path.

This first verse frames the idea that society has rules and that the rules should be followed by everyone. Thus, while someone might be idly daydreaming on a patch of grass, being off the beaten path is frowned upon, and there may be a keep-off-the-grass sign to be reckoned with. There is a societal impulse to have people remain in the fold, to conform to expected roles, and pressures are brought to bear on those who are out of step or off the path.

The trivial nature of being off the path in the first verse gives the impression that "Brain Damage" may be limited to unobjectionable, non-violent aspects of mental illness, a limit mostly respected by the balance of the song. "Brain Damage" seems to say that while efforts will be made to keep the mentally ill in line when they impact society, there will be an uneasy tolerance of them, or, rather, a turning of a blind eye to them, so long as they keep their illness to themselves and do not impact others too much.

The next verse, however, does bring the mentally ill into closer and closer contact, first into your own building, and then into your own hall, first just one, and then more:

The lunatic is in the hall.

The lunatics are in my hall.

There is a chuckle beneath these lines as well, in this case adding a certain unstable intimacy to the lyrics. The verse goes on to say that while they may indeed be physically proximate, the mentally ill are also nearby in a more figurative sense — in the newspaper, for example:

The paper holds their folded faces to the floor

And every day the paper boy brings more.

"Normal" people's stories do not get told in the newspaper. Newspapers have long — perhaps always — been associated more closely with the lurid and unfortunate than the beneficial and charmed. Notoriously, the worse or the stranger the story, the more likely it may be to wind up on the front page. When the person has done something crazy enough, or had something terrible enough happen to him or her, a front-page picture of them may accompany their story, to be folded and set by your doorstep each morning or afternoon. And, it seems, every day has its share of mysterious deaths, suicides, overdoses, public fallings-out, embarrassing photos, outbursts and overreactions.

38. The way the papers were often delivered *holds their folded faces to the floor / and every day the paper boy brings more.*

These lines resonate very strongly with Don McLean's 1971 hit "American Pie," about the deaths in an airplane crash of Buddy Holly, Ritchie Valens, and J.P. Richardson, also known as "the Big Bopper."

> *But February made me shiver*
>
> *With every paper I'd deliver*
>
> *Bad news on the doorstep*
>
> *I couldn't take one more step*[223]

Those deaths occurred more than a decade before "American Pie" was released, reflecting just how deeply McLean had been affected by the loss of these Rock 'n' Roll pioneers.

---

[223] Gur Tirosh, "The Complete True Story Behind 'American Pie' by Don McLean," History by day (History by Day, October 7, 2019), https://www.historybyday.com/human-stories/the-complete-true-story-behind-american-pie-by-don-mclean/.

39. This 2014 photograph, taken by Carol Highsmith, is of the statue of rock-'n'-roll legend Buddy Holly erected in Holly's hometown of Lubbock, Texas, and is courtesy of the Library of Congress. https://www.loc.gov/item/2014633889/.

In a similar vein, in the few years while *The Dark Side of the Moon* was germinating, the deaths of many other famous personalities in the music world filled the news:

Janis Joplin died October 4, 1970, of a heroin overdose.[224]

Jimi Hendrix died September 18, 1970, choking on vomit after taking barbiturates.[225]

[224] Biography.com Editors, "Janis Joplin Biography," The Biography.com (A&E Television Networks, April 4, 2014), https://www.biography.com/people/janis-joplin.

[225] Rolling Stone, "Hendrix Inquest Inconclusive Not Enough Evidence to Say for Sure What Motives Were behind Jimi's Death," *Rolling Stone* (Penske Business Media, LLC,

Jim Morrison died July 3, 1971, ostensibly from natural causes, but with foam around his mouth.[226]

Alan Wilson of Canned Heat, best known as the idiosyncratic lead singer of "On the Road Again," died September 3, 1970, of a barbiturate overdose.[227]

Billy Murcia, original drummer for the New York Dolls, died on November 6, 1972, overdosing on drugs and alcohol and apparently being suffocated by black coffee as his girlfriend tried to keep him alive.[228]

Looking more deeply into these front-page stories often reveals that problems have been accumulating for years, until some additional stress crosses some hidden threshold, some last straw breaks the camel's back. "Brain Damage" mirrors this idea. With a building crescendo, the inability to contain and maintain madness within limits is dramatically underscored by the swelling sound of the chorus, drums and cymbals:

> *And if the dam breaks open many years too soon*
>
> *And if there is no room upon the hill*
>
> *And if your head explodes with dark forebodings too*
>
> *I'll see you on the dark side of the moon.*

That a chorus accompanies these lines may be in part to echo the idea that *there is no room upon the hill*, that there is a crowd, if only in one's head. The phrase *room upon the hill* itself likely refers to the Beatles' 1967 song "The Fool On The Hill," which had similar themes of societal disapproval and the separate, internal world of the mentally ill:

> *Day after day, alone on a hill*
>
> *The man with the foolish grin is sitting perfectly still*
>
> *Nobody wants to know him*
>
> *They can see that he's just a fool*
>
> *But he never gives an answer*
>
> *But the fool on the hill*

June 25, 2018), https://www.rollingstone.com/music/news/hendrix-inquest-inconclusive-19701029.

[226] Elizabeth Goodman, "Jim Morrison's Death May Be Reinvestigated," *Rolling Stone* (Penske Business Media, LLC., June 25, 2018), https://www.rollingstone.com/music/news/jim-morrisons-death-may-be-reinvestigated-20070710.

[227] Dave Lifton, "Alan Wilson of Canned Heat Rockers Who Died at Age 27," Ultimate Classic Rock (Townsquare Media, Inc., August 22, 2013), https://ultimateclassicrock.com/alan-wilson-rockers-who-died-at-age-27.

[228] Reginald Reginald, "Billy Dolls Murcia (1951–1972) — Find A Grave...," Find a Grave (Ancestry, July 21, 2006), https://www.findagrave.com/memorial/15004578/billy-dolls-murcia.

Sees the sun going down

And the eyes in his head

See the world spinning round[229]

In contrast to the inspiration of a mentally unstable Syd Barrett, when Paul McCartney wrote "The Fool On The Hill," he had the idea that someone commonly believed to be a fool may indeed be quite wise, akin to features of the archetypal Trickster. McCartney specifically had in mind Maharishi Mahesh Yogi, an Indian guru The Beatles met in 1967. The Beatles learned Transcendental Meditation from him, and even visited him in India in 1968.[230]

"The Fool on the Hill" presents a peaceful, almost idyllic world, whether for those who had renounced the world or the mentally ill. Like the hill in "The Fool on the Hill," "Brain Damage" presents the dark side of the moon as a refuge for those who no longer belong within the customary confines of civilization. For as long as there has been civilization, there seems to have been fantasies of an ideal place, but a place that is never here.

Like the island in Sir Thomas More's 1516 tale *Utopia*, or the hidden village of Shangri-La in James Hilton's 1933 novel *Lost Horizons*, or even Pepperland from The Beatles' movie *Yellow Submarine*, the dark side of the moon is separate from the rest of the world. The dark side of the moon is remote and mysterious, free of people who would judge someone for being different.

To Cut or To Cage

The next verse of "Brain Damage," accompanied by a much more distinct, exuberant, and less controlled laugh, chronicles some of this darkness and the reaction to it:

The lunatic is in my head.

The lunatic is in my head

You raise the blade, you make the change

You re-arrange me 'til I'm sane.

You lock the door

And throw away the key

There's someone in my head but it's not me.

---

[229] Beatles Lyrics: The Fool on the Hill (BeatlesLyrics.org, 2008), https://www.beatles-lyrics.org/index_files/Page7228.htm.

[230] Joe Goodden, "Maharishi Mahesh Yogi," The Beatles Bible, June 8, 2020, https://www.beatlesbible.com/people/maharishi-mahesh-yogi.

40. This trading card from the late nineteenth century depicts The Utopias of Air Navigation of the Last Century, one of ten Collecting Cards With Pictures of Events in Ballooning History from 1795 to 1846, in the Tissandier Collection at the Library of Congress. [Paris: Romanet & cie., imp. edit., between 1890 and 1900]. https://www.loc.gov/item/2002717347/.

These lines reflect two interventions — lobotomy (*raise the blade*) and institutionalization (*lock the door*) — that were among the most severe treatments given to the mentally ill. While institutionalization has a history measured in centuries,[231] lobotomies were a product of the 1930s.[232] The

---

[231] See, e.g., David J. Rothman, *The Discovery of the Asylum: Social Order and Disorder in the New Republic* (London: Routledge, 2017).

[232] Tanya Lewis, "Lobotomy: Definition, Procedure & History," LiveScience (Future US, Inc., August 29, 2014), https://www.livescience.com/42199-lobotomy-definition.html.

lobotomy was very much a literal rearrangement of the brain, as can be seen vividly from an excerpt of a 1942 medical presentation:[233]

> When the surgeon is satisfied with his landmarks, he clamps a hemostat on the shaft of a blunt knife (we use Killian's nasal septum periosteal elevator) and introduces the instrument to a depth short of the midline (beware the anterior cerebral artery!) and begins the fanlike incisions in the frontal lobe (Fig. 2). During this procedure the neurologist guides the surgeon, keeping the knife and the' hemostat both in the plane of the coronal suture, by means of constantly correcting the surgeon's tendency to deviate from this plane. The depth of the incision must be judged by the surgeon, any increased resistance being the signal for withdrawing the instrument as a precaution against lacerating an artery. Once the primary incision has been made, it is safe to deepen the incision by radial thrusts of the knife that will push any intruding artery before it and at the same time reach the more peripheral parts of the white matter in the frontal poles.

As brutal as this process may sound, at the time of its introduction there was no other effective treatment for schizophrenia, severe anxiety, and compulsive syndromes. The doctor who developed the method, Egas Moniz, won the Nobel Prize for it in 1949.[234]

Development of treatments for schizophrenia was critical, as by the middle of the twentieth century its clinical definition made clear how severe the problem could be:[235]

> Symptoms such as hallucinations and delusions, considered secondary by Bleuler, became the foremost defining criteria, and special forms such as voices commenting on behavior or discussing the patient in third person pronouns became critical to the diagnosis of schizophrenia.

The Bleuler referred above to is Paul Eugen Bleuler, who coined the word schizophrenia in 1908.[236] It is interesting to note that Carl Jung, who attributed the development of his theory of archetypes in part to observations of

[233] Walter Freeman and James W Watts, "Prefrontal Lobotomy: The Surgical Relief of Mental Pain," National Center for Biotechnology Information (U.S. National Library of Medicine, October 22, 1942), https://www.ncbi.nlm.nih.gov/pmc/articles/PMC1933933/pdf/bullnyacadmed00561-0025.pdf, pp. 797-799.

[234] Bengt Jansson, "Controversial Psychosurgery Resulted in a Nobel Prize," NobelPrize.org (Nobel Media AB, October 29, 1998), https://www.nobelprize.org/nobel_prizes/medicine/laureates/1949/moniz-article.html.

[235] William T Carpenter and James I Koenig, "The Evolution of Drug Development in Schizophrenia: Past Issues and Future Opportunities," Nature News (Nature Publishing Group, November 28, 2007), https://www.nature.com/articles/1301639.

[236] Paolo Fusar-Poli and Pierluigi Politi, "Paul Eugen Bleuler and the Birth of Schizophrenia (1908)," The American Journal of Psychiatry (U.S. National Library of Medicine, November 2008), http://www.ncbi.nlm.nih.gov/pubmed/18981075.

schizophrenic patients, was Bleuler's assistant at the Psychiatrische Univer-
sitätsklinik Zürich (Psychiatric University Hospital Zürich).[237]

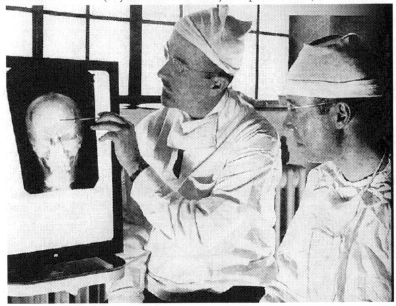

41. This public-domain photograph, taken by Harris A Ewing, from the
May 24, 1941, *Saturday Evening Post*, shows, "Dr. Walter Freeman, left, and Dr.
James W. Watts study an X ray before a psychosurgical operation. Psychosurgery is cutting into the brain to form new patterns and rid a patient of
delusions, obsessions, nervous tensions and the like."

From the 1950s forward, pharmaceutical treatments for schizophrenia
began to be introduced and the use of lobotomies began to wane over
time. Institutionalization in mental hospitals for years at a time continued,
however. In 1959, there were 535,000 patients in public mental hospitals in
the United States, of whom approximately 50% were schizophrenic.[238]

In a survey of the medical literature published in *Scientific American* in
August 1962, Don D. Jackson, director of the Mental Research Institute of
the Palo Alto Medical Research Foundation and associate clinical professor
of psychiatry at the Stanford University School of Medicine, observed:[239]

---

[237] Stephan Heckers, "Bleuler and the Neurobiology of Schizophrenia," *Schizophrenia Bulletin*
(Oxford University Press, November 2011), https://www.ncbi.nlm.nih.gov/pmc/articles/
PMC3196934.
[238] Don D. Jackson, "Schizophrenia," in *Frontiers of Psychological Research: Readings from
Scientific American*, selected by S. Coopersmith (and Company, San Francisco and London:
W. H. Freeman 1966), pp. 288-89.
[239] *Id.*, p. 285.

The diagnosis of schizophrenia accounts for more than half of the mentally ill patients who fill more than half of the hospital beds in this country [the U.S.]. Typically the disorder overtakes younger people — "between the ages of 18 and 28." Often it maims them for life: The schizophrenic entering a state hospital has little better than an even chance of ever returning to society as a functioning member.

While it was not as common as it was in the 1950s, by the mid-1970s there were still on the order of 200,000 people in state mental hospitals.[240]

Though many patients had been released from institutionalization, the consequences thereof were mixed: Because many mentally ill outside of hospitals do not receive adequate ongoing care, there are more than three times as many seriously mentally ill people in jails and prisons than in hospitals.[241] That is, one way or another, whether asylum or jail cell, the outcome is much the same:

You lock the door

And throw away the key

There's someone in my head but it's not me.

"Brain Damage" was deeply personal for the members of Pink Floyd, referring obliquely to their experiences with Pink Floyd's founding member, Syd Barrett.

Barrett's influence on the band and legacy were profound. Barrett named the band — which at the time was comprised of Roger Waters on bass, Rick Wright on keyboards, and Nick Mason on drums — The Pink Floyd Sound, after two blues musicians, Pink Anderson and Floyd Council, whom he'd read about on a record sleeve.[242] Barrett was also the key figure behind Pink Floyd's 1967 album *The Piper at the Gates of Dawn*, which contained much that was psychedelic, including the songs "Astronomy Domine" and "Interstellar Overdrive," which the band continued to perform live for decades after Barrett was no longer in the band.

---

[240] Ann E. P Dill, *Managing to Care: Case Management and Service System Reform* (New York: Aldine de Gruyter, 2001), p. 78 (citing *The President's Commission on Mental Illness*, vol.1, 1978).

[241] Kimberly Amadeo, "Deinstitutionalization, Its Causes, Effects, Pros and Cons: How Deinstitutionalization in the 1970s Affects You Today," The Balance (Dotdash, September 24, 2020), https://www.thebalance.com/deinstitutionalization-3306067.

[242] David Cavanagh, "The Glory and Torment of Being Syd Barrett, by David Bowie, David Gilmour, Mick Rock, Joe Boyd, Damon Albarn and More...," *UNCUT* (BandLab Technologies, January 24, 2014), http://www.uncut.co.uk/features/the-glory-and-torment-of-being-syd-barrett-by-david-bowie-david-gilmour-mick-rock-joe-boyd-damon-albarn-and-more-13127.

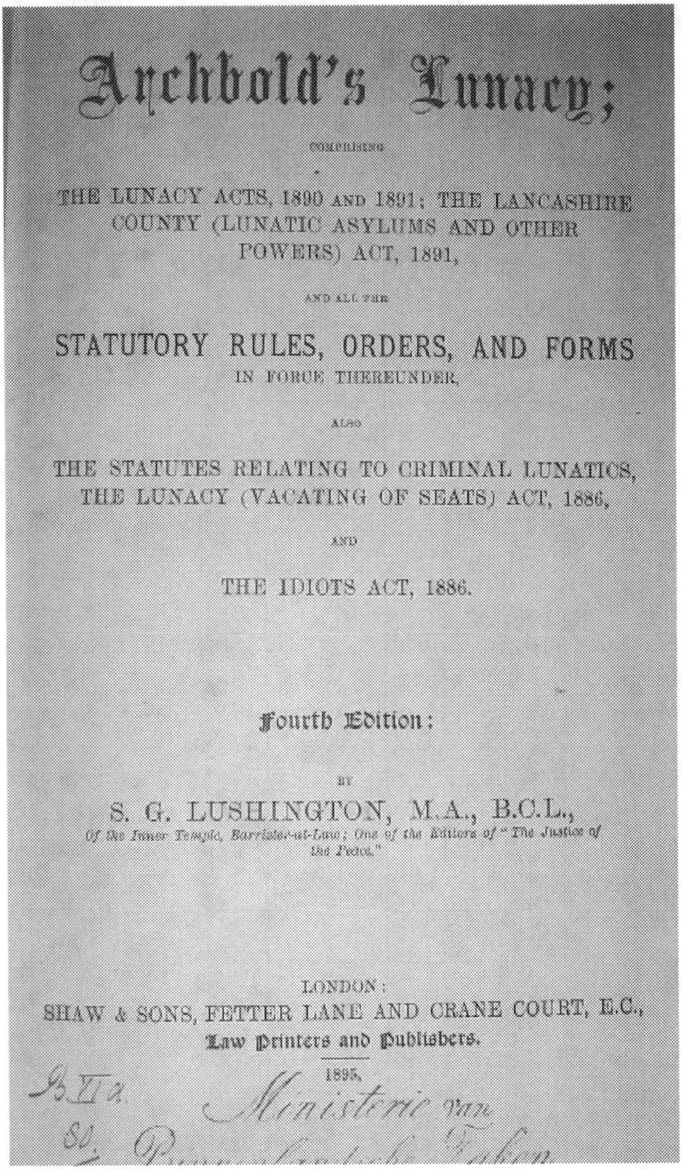

Archbold's Lunacy;

COMPRISING

THE LUNACY ACTS, 1890 AND 1891; THE LANCASHIRE
COUNTY (LUNATIC ASYLUMS AND OTHER
POWERS) ACT, 1891,

AND ALL THE

STATUTORY RULES, ORDERS, AND FORMS
IN FORCE THEREUNDER,

ALSO

THE STATUTES RELATING TO CRIMINAL LUNATICS,
THE LUNACY (VACATING OF SEATS) ACT, 1886,

AND

THE IDIOTS ACT, 1886.

Fourth Edition:

BY

S. G. LUSHINGTON, M.A., B.C.L.,
*Of the Inner Temple, Barrister-at-Law; One of the Editors of "The Justice of
the Peace."*

LONDON:
SHAW & SONS, FETTER LANE AND CRANE COURT, E.C.,
Law Printers and Publishers.

1895.

42. Prior to the development of medical interventions, the laws for maintaining institutionalized patients ran to more than 900 pages in the United Kingdom. Shown here is the 1895 collection of laws, *Archbold's lunacy: comprising the Lunacy Acts, 1890 and 1891; the Lancashire County (Lunatic Asylums and Other Powers) Act, 1891, and all the statutory rules, orders and forms in force thereunder, also the statutes relating to criminal lunatics, the Lunacy (Vacating of Seats) Act, 1886, and the Idiots Act, 1886.* Photograph by the author.

It would be tempting to view Barrett's behavior as that of the archetypal Trickster, like the one whom the author and screenwriting consultant Linda Seger described succinctly as "a mischievous archetypical figure who is always causing chaos, disturbing the peace, and generally being an anarchist."[243] Given that the chaos, disruption, and anarchy around Barrett seemed to take a progressive toll on him, however, it calls to mind the observation made by the philosopher and social/political theorist and critic Herbert Marcuse in his most influential book, *Eros and Civilization: A Philosophical Inquiry Into Freud:*[244]

> [W]e look for the "culture-heroes" who have persisted in imagination as symbolizing the attitude and the deeds that have determined the fate of mankind. And here at the outset we are confronted with the fact that the predominant culture-hero is the trickster and (suffering) rebel against the gods, who creates culture at the price of perpetual pain.

Despite his genius, Barrett had become progressively more difficult to work with. During the recording of *The Piper at the Gates of Dawn*, Barrett was increasingly filled with psychedelics.[245] Anecdotes of his behavior show how deeply his behavior had deteriorated, and how vividly people around him recalled it. For example, the band's co-manager Peter Jenner described how his behavior was strange, even accounting for his drug use:[246]

> During that summer ['67], Syd was becoming increasingly difficult. At some of the UFO gigs, he'd play one note all night. Even though he was tripping on acid, I thought that was odd behaviour . . .

As bad as this was, things became worse. June Bolan, wife of Marc Bolan, the gifted guitarist of Tyrannosaurus Rex and T. Rex, had actually dated Syd Barrett and attended the last show in which Barrett took the stage. He did not exactly perform, however. When the band was supposed to take the stage, Barrett was not around. She found him in the dressing room, catatonic. Roger Waters helped her get him onto the stage and put a guitar around his

---

[243] Linda Seger, "Creating the Myth," in Sonia Maasik and Jack Solomon, eds., *Signs of Life in the USA: Readings on Popular Culture for Writers* (Boston: Bedford/St Martins, 2011), p. 393.

[244] Herbert Marcuse, *Eros and Civilization: A Philosophical Inquiry into Freud* (Boston: Beacon Press, 1955), p. 161.

[245] Andrew O'Brien, "Remembering The Troubled Genius Of Syd Barrett On 'The Piper At The Gates Of Dawn'," L4LM, January 6, 2020, https://liveforlivemusic.com/features/pink-floyd-piper-gates-dawn-1967.

[246] David Cavanagh, "The Glory and Torment of Being Syd Barrett, by David Bowie, David Gilmour, Mick Rock, Joe Boyd, Damon Albarn and More..."

neck. When the rest of the band began to play, Barrett just stood there while the rest of the band played.[247]

A few years later, this episode illuminated the last verse of "Brain Damage," where the music again surges, with cymbal crashes to emphasize the internal violence of a mental breakdown:

And if the cloud bursts, thunder in your ear

You shout and no one seems to hear.

And if the band you're in starts playing different tunes

I'll see you on the dark side of the moon.

The chorus that swells with the surge in music that begins with this verse gives greater emotional depth to these more personal lines. Just as *You shout and no one seems to hear* is being sung, moreover, a female backing voice soars above the chorus of voices that had been accompanying the lead. This very brief solo mirrors the *shout*, and emphasizes the aloneness conveyed by this verse. A different solo excursion of *hey-hey-hey* underpins *And if the band you're in starts playing different tunes*, subtly evoking the idea of a separate song. The background voices fall silent through the next verse.

The psychology researcher and teacher Julian Jaynes used remarkably similar imagery to describe the effects of hearing voices has on some schizophrenics:[248]

> The anxiety attendant upon so cataclysmic a change, the dissonance with the habitual structure of interpersonal relations, and the lack of cultural support and definition for the voices, making them inadequate guides for everyday living, the need to defend against a broken dam of environmental sensory stimulation that is flooding all before it — produce a social withdrawal that is a far different thing from the behavior of the absolutely social individual of bicameral societies.

The reference in the last phrase of this excerpt refers directly to Jaynes' thesis in his book *The Origins of Consciousness in the Breakdown of the Bicameral Mind*. While fairly controversial — so much so that that part of the Julian Jaynes Society website is expressly devoted to addressing criticisms of the theory,[249] — Jaynes' theory was based on his own original analysis of history and many cultural developments, particularly ancient Greek mythology, music and poetry.

---

[247] June Child, "Life with Syd Barrett," Bolan World, June 8, 2017, https://mistymist.wordpress.com/discography/ride-a-white-swan/june-child/.

[248] Jaynes, *The Origins of Consciousness*, p. 432.

[249] Marcel Kuijsten, "Ten Questions Critics Fail to Answer About Julian Jaynes's Theory," Julian Jaynes Society, October 28, 2019, https://www.julianjaynes.org/blog/julian-jaynes-theory/ten-questions-critics-fail-to-answer-about-julian-jayness-theory.

Jaynes asserts that people were not always able to perform introspection or self-visualization, which are what he uses as the signposts of consciousness, and that these are relatively recent phenomena, dating only from around the time of the composition of *The Iliad*.

In *The "bicameral mind" 30 years on: a critical reappraisal of Julian Jaynes' hypothesis*,[250] four respected psychologists from the University of Bologna and Amedeo Avogadro University in Italy and the Institute of Neurology in London carefully examined his theory and addressed two main areas of criticism, the neurological basis of the bicameral model and the accuracy of Jaynes' arguments related to the structure, historical development, and relationships of languages.

While not embracing the theory as such, this reappraisal did show that Jaynes' non-unitary concept of the Self coincides with more recent findings from cognitive neuroscience studies. For example, Bernard Baars, co-founder of the Association for the Scientific Study of Consciousness,[251] hypothesized a "global workspace theory" in which consciousness emerges as a result of integrated activity among diverse unconscious brain processes.[252] Ultimately, as summarized in an abstract of *The "bicameral mind" 30 years on*, prepared by the National Center for Biotechnology Information, "the concept of a non-unitary Self is presented as one of the most relevant contemporary legacies of the bicameral mind."[253]

While Jaynes wrote above of schizophrenia, a description also evoking the *And if the cloud bursts, thunder in your ear / You shout and no one seems to hear* lyrics may be found in *Darkness Visible*, the first-person account of the writer William Styron's battle with profound depression:

> But never let it be doubted that depression, in its extreme form, is madness. The madness results from an aberrant biochemical process. It has been established with reasonable certainty (after strong resistance from many psychiatrists, and not all that long ago) that such madness is chemically induced amid the neurotransmitters of the brain, probably as the result of systemic stress, which for unknown reasons causes a depletion of the chemicals norepinephrine and serotonin, and the increase of a hormone, cortisol. With all of this upheaval

[250]Andrea Eugenio Cavanna, Michael Trimble, Frederico Cinti, and Francesco Monaco (2007). "The "bicameral mind" 30 years on: a critical reappraisal of Julian Jaynes' hypothesis." *Functional Neurology*, 22(1), 11—15, https://pubmed.ncbi.nlm.nih.gov/17509238.

[251]"Past Leadership," theASSC.org (Association For The Scientific Study Of Consciousness, 2020), https://theassc.org/past-leadership.

[252] Bernard J Baars, "The Global Workspace Theory of Consciousness," Wiley Online Library (John Wiley & Sons, Ltd, March 17, 2017), https://onlinelibrary.wiley.com/doi/10.1002/9781119132363.ch16.

[253] A.E. Cavanna, et al., The "bicameral mind" 30 years on, https://www.ncbi.nlm.nih.gov/pubmed/17509238.

in the brain tissues, the alternate drenching and deprivation, it is no wonder that the mind begins to feel aggrieved, stricken, and the muddied thought processes register the distress of an organ in convulsion. Sometimes, though not very often, such a disturbed mind will turn to violent thoughts regarding others. But with their minds turned agonizingly inward, people with depression are usually dangerous only to themselves. The madness of depression is, generally speaking, the antithesis of violence. It is a storm indeed, but a storm of murk.[254]

Recalling the lines *The paper holds their folded faces to the floor / And every day the paper boy brings more*, Styron catalogues many of the famous and talented whom depression gripped:

Despite depression's eclectic reach, it has demonstrated with fair convincingness that artistic types (especially poets) are particularly vulnerable to the disorder — which in its graver, clinical manifestation takes upward of 20 percent of its victims by way of suicide. Just a few of these fallen artists, all modern, make up a sad but scintillant roll call: Hart Crane, Vincent Van Gogh, Virginia Woolf, Arshile Gorky, Cesare Pavese, Romain Gary, Sylvia Plath, Mark Rothko, John Berryman, Jack London, Ernest Hemingway, Diane Arbus, Tadeusz Borowski, Paul Celan, Anne Sexton, Sergei Esenin, Vladimir Mayakovsky—the list goes on.[255]

Though not suicidal, it did seem clear that Syd Barrett was no longer mentally intact. The guitarist David Gilmour had by this time been brought into the band, initially with the thought that he would supplement the band. But as Barrett continued to deteriorate, it quickly became clear that Gilmour would supplant, rather than supplement, Barrett. As described by Gilmour, the decision to cut Barrett from the band was very spur of the moment, actually on the way to a show. One person in the car asked if they should pick Syd up, and another simply said not to.[256]

And so, Syd Barrett is left behind as the band he formed moved forward, left on his own dark side of the moon.

After Pink Floyd, Barrett continued intermittently to work on music for a few years. His 1970 debut solo work, *The Madcap Laughs*, seems very much the work of, or a homage to, the Trickster. Though an uncomfortable effort for many listeners, others hear *The Madcap Laughs* as a distinct work of genius.[257] He followed it with one more solo album, called simply *Barrett*, before leaving

---

[254] William Styron, *Darkness Visible* (New York: Random House, 1992), pp. 46-47.

[255] *Id.*, pp. 35-36.

[256] Alan di Perna, "David's Harp," in *Guitar World Presents Pink Floyd*, pp. 54-55.

[257] *See, e.g.*, Ed Prideaux, "You Feel Me: Syd Barrett and The Madcap Laughs," *Cultural Weekly* (Next Echo Foundation, July 11, 2018), https://www.culturalweekly.com/feel-syd-barrett-madcap-laughs.

the music world to live in his mother's basement in Cambridge.[258] This destiny seems to embody an observation by the author Sallie Nichols:[259]

> The Fool, be he court jester, trickster, or circus clown, is always touched with the sadness and loneliness of any figure who stands outside the cozy anonymity enjoyed by the average man.

After declaring that *I'll see you on the dark side of the moon*, "Brain Damage" continues instrumentally for another 45 seconds or so, and while it is very similar to how the song began, the drummed heartbeat is gone. About twenty seconds into this instrumental interval, an unidentified voice is heard to say, *I can't think of anything to say except…* And the unhinged laughter returns, seemingly from someone other than the first speaker. After a few moments, the first voice says, *I think it's marvelous!* and breaks into its own laugh.

The complete absence of context for these two snatches of conversation, along with the laughter from each of the speakers, fits the disconnectedness conveyed by the balance of the song. "Brain Damage" then ends, with its last few seconds merged with the beginning of "Eclipse," with four solid bass drum beats making the bridge.

Track Eleven: Eclipse

Strong drumming by Nick Mason dominates the musical support of the recitation of catalogue of living a life given in "Eclipse":

> *All that you touch*
> *All that you see*
> *All that you taste*
> *All you feel.*
> *All that you love*
> *All that you hate*
> *All you distrust*
> *All you save.*
> *All that you give*
> *All that you deal*
> *All that you buy,*
> *beg, borrow or steal.*
> *All you create*
> *All you destroy*

---

[258] *Id.*
[259] Sallie Nichols, *Jung and Tarot*, p. 36.

All that you do

All that you say.

All that you eat

And everyone you meet

All that you slight

And everyone you fight.

All that is now

All that is gone

All that's to come

and everything under the sun is in tune

but the sun is eclipsed by the moon.

Coming at the end of the album, the words of "Eclipse" make a tremendous impression. The lyrics are sung in only about a minute and a half, but weave together the many themes and thoughts of the rest of the album in a manifesto of sorts. The female chorus joins in at *All that you love*, though, adding a mystical overtone.

It could be said that it is Pink Floyd's answer to the Buddha's Noble Eightfold Path, which the Buddha had articulated as a means to free oneself from worldly attachments and delusions. A very brief overview of what the Noble Eightfold Path is provided by the Society for the Promotion of Buddhism, Bukkyo Dendō Kyōkai, in "The Way of Practical Attainment" chapter of *The Teaching of Buddha*:

The Noble Eightfold Path refers to:

right view,

right thought,

right speech,

right behavior,

right livelihood,

right effort,

right mindfulness, and

right concentration.[260]

Each of the practices of the Eightfold Path has its own doctrine, elucidation, and practice, but at least some of their usefulness and impact is from their conciseness, directness, and simplicity, allowing them to be fully

---

[260] *The Teaching of Buddha* (Tokyo, Japan: Bukkyo Dendō Kyōkai, 2002), pp. 166-67 (format altered by the author).

integrated into one's daily life. They are a sort of spiritual shorthand. The Eightfold Path is an important part of the teachings of the Buddha, laying out fundamental, yet practical, principles to guide the elimination of suffering in life, an easily remembered guide to much more expansive teaching:[261]

> Right View means to thoroughly understand the Fourfold Truth, to believe in the law of cause and effect and not to be deceived by appearances and desires.

> Right Thought means the resolution not to cherish desires, not to be greedy, not to be angry, and not to do any harmful deed.

> Right Speech means the avoidance of lying words, idle words, abusive words, and double-tongues.

> Right Behavior means not to destroy any life, not to steal, or not to commit adultery.

> Right Livelihood means to avoid any life that would bring shame.

> Right Effort means to try to do one's best diligently toward the right direction.

> Right Mindfulness means to maintain a pure and thoughtful mind.

> Right Concentration means to keep the mind right and tranquil for its concentration, seeking to realize the mind's pure essence.

The Fourfold Truth referred to in the Right View description is also called the Four Noble Truths, and is the cornerstone of Buddhism. These came about through Siddhartha Gautama, who had been born into a rich family, but gave it up to wander across India. As Peter Matthiessen tells it in *The Snow Leopard*, Gautama became known as Sakyamuni, or Sage of the Sakya clan, and then Buddha, or the Awakened One, whose experiences led him to a deep realization:[262]

> In what became known as the Four Noble Truths, Sakyamuni perceived that man's existence is inseparable from sorrow; that the cause of suffering is craving; that peace is attained by extinguishing craving; that this liberation may be brought about by following the Eight-fold Path: right attention to one's understanding, intentions, speech, and actions; right livelihood, effort, mindfulness; right concentration, by which is meant the unification of the self through sitting yoga.

As may be obvious from just these couple of observations, the specific phrasing of and doctrinal details and nuance of the Four Noble Truths and the Eightfold Path differ somewhat for different Buddhist sects, but are nonetheless fundamental across all Buddhism.

---

[261] *Id.*
[262] Peter Matthiessen, *The Snow Leopard*, pp. 17–18.

A similar set of guidelines was provided by Jesus Christ, in the Beatitudes delivered in the Sermon on the Mount. One of the most familiar teachings of Jesus, the Beatitudes set out several qualities which exemplify blessedness, giving clear guidance to how to live a good life. They are, as set forth by his Apostle, Matthew:

43. 1908 Buddha photograph by Arnold Genthe, from Travel views of Japan and Korea, Genthe photograph collection, Library of Congress. http://loc.gov/pictures/resource/agc.7a04544/.

44. 1866 Currier & Ives lithograph of *Christ's Sermon on the Mount: The Parable of the Lily* is courtesy Library of Congress. [New York: Currier & Ives] https://www.loc.gov/item/90715956/.

Blessed are the poor in spirit: for theirs is the kingdom of heaven.

Blessed are they that mourn: for they shall be comforted.

Blessed are the meek: for they shall inherit the earth.

Blessed are they which do hunger and thirst after righteousness: for they shall be filled.

Blessed are the merciful: for they shall obtain mercy.

Blessed are the pure in heart: for they shall see God.

Blessed are the peacemakers: for they shall be called the children of God.

Blessed are they which are persecuted for righteousness' sake: for theirs is the kingdom of heaven.

Blessed are ye, when men shall revile you, and persecute you, and shall say all manner of evil against you falsely, for my sake.[263]

[263] Matt 5:3—12, "Bible Gateway Passage: Matthew 5 — King James Version," Bible Gateway (Good News Publishers), accessed November 22, 2020, https://www.biblegateway.com/passage/?search=Matthew+5&version=KJV.

Each of these Beatitudes speaks to those in need of comfort, and provides a concise aspirational guide to how a life according to Christ's teaching could be led.

A Different Kind of Comfort

"Eclipse" offers a slightly different kind of comfort, though. It does not offer Nirvana or Heaven, as such, but does nonetheless hold a promise of something more than what is reflected in its bare recitation of elements of a life (*but the sun is eclipsed by the moon*). In that regard, it is a response to or even a repudiation of the flat statement in "Breathe:"

Long you live and high you fly

And smiles you'll give and tears you'll cry

And all you touch and all you see

Is all your life will ever be.

The *all your life will ever be* statement in "Breathe" is existential in nature, in that it clearly states that life is what you make it, and its meaning is what you give it. There is nothing outside, above, or hereafter to grant purpose to a life which its owner had not. As Jean-Paul Sartre had articulated in his 1945 speech, "Existentialism is a Humanism," human beings do not have a role, use or function endowed upon them, as if they were a book or a scissors created for a particular purpose, but must instead create that essence him- or herself:[264]

> We mean that man first exists: he materializes in the world, encounters himself, and only afterward defines himself. If man as existentialists conceive of him cannot be defined, it is because to begin with he is nothing. He will not be anything until later, and then he will be what he makes of himself.

In a passage very like a verse from "Breathe," Sartre states:[265]

> Man is nothing other than his own project. He exists only to the extent that he realizes himself, therefore he is nothing more than the sum of his actions, nothing more than his life."

As a person is wholly responsible for her- or himself and what becomes of her or him, it means that the weight and meaning given to the choices made and the experiences that flow from those choices are also wholly up to the individual. In illustrating just how far he believes this responsibility extends,

---

[264] Jean-Paul Sartre, "[Jean Paul Sartre] Existentialism Is A Humanism(z Lib.org)," ed. John Kulka, trans. Carol Macomber, Internet Archive (Yale University Press, December 20, 2019), https://archive.org/details/jeanpaulsartreexistentialismisahumanismzlib.org, p. 22.

[265] *Id.*, p. 37.

Sartre hearkens back to Kierkegaard's discussion of Abraham being told by God to kill his own son:[266]

> You know the story: an angel orders Abraham to sacrifice his son. This would be okay provided it is really an angel who appears to him and says, "Thou, Abraham, shalt sacrifice thy son." But any sane person may wonder first whether it is truly an angel, and second, whether I am really Abraham. What proof do I have? There was once a mad woman suffering from hallucinations who claimed that people were phoning her and giving her orders. The doctor asked her, "But who exactly speaks to you?" She replied, "He says it is God." How did she actually know for certain that it was God? If an angel appears to me, what proof do I have that it is an angel? Or if I hear voices, what proof is there that they come from heaven and not from hell, or from my own subconscious, or some pathological condition? What proof is there that they are intended for me? What proof is there that I am the proper person to impose my conception of man on humanity? I will never find any proof at all, nor any convincing sign of it. If a voice speaks to me, it is always I who must decide whether or not this is the voice of an angel; if I regard a certain course of action as good, it is I who will choose to say that it is good, rather than bad.

It is a very challenging philosophy of life, literally, which is unforgiving to those who stand by and wish their life were different:[267]

> No doubt this thought may seem harsh to someone who has not made a success of his life. But on the other hand, it helps people to understand that reality alone counts, and that dreams, expectations, and hopes only serve to define a man as a broken dream, aborted hopes, and futile expectations; in other words, they define him negatively, not positively. Nonetheless, saying "You are nothing but your life" does not imply that the artist will be judged solely by his works of art, for a thousand other things also help to define him. What we mean to say is that a man is nothing but a series of enterprises, and that he is the sum, organization, and aggregate of the relations that constitute such enterprises.

In similar manner, "Eclipse" focuses on actions, embracing the physical (*touch/see/taste/feel*), the emotional (*love/hate/distrust*), the economic (*give/deal/buy/beg/borrow/steal*), the constructive (*create/destroy*), and the social (*do/say/eat/meet/slight/fight*), comprehending many of the main ways people fill their time to construct their lives. But "Eclipse" is suggestive, and is not comprehensive.

For example, although *All that you give, all that you deal* is included with *All that you buy, beg, borrow or steal*, this list notably omits what may be given to you. But what may be given to you is a choice someone else is making, not

---

[266] *Id.*, p. 25-26.
[267] *Id.*, p. 38.

a choice you make, insofar as to receive something may be viewed as essentially a passive engagement. Hence, as it is not in your control, it should not be in this particular list. This is a bit weak, however, inasmuch as whether one accepts something that another is attempting to give them is definitely a personal decision.

That the phrase *All that you give* is repeated by a solo singer breaking away from the chorus does not clarify this conundrum. Perhaps it is simply to emphasize the importance of giving. But this vocal excursion is the beginning of a cascade of additional solo flights accompanying the chorus. These are mainly non-verbal, though *everyone you meet* is the only one that uses words. While these outpourings may not have a denotative meaning, they do call to mind the soaring flights of "The Great Gig in the Sky."

Though perhaps not complete, in this succinct litany, "Eclipse" shows how rich even a simple life can be, if one is fully conscious of these many actions. It is like the realization made by the central character Meursault in Albert Camus' 1967 novel *The Stranger*, only after he has been put into a cell:[268]

> So I learned after a single day's experience of the outside world a man could easily live a hundred years in prison. He'd have laid up enough memories never to be bored.

"Eclipse" also addresses time itself (*now/gone/to come*). This manifests the panorama in which lives are made. It would be useful here to recall the discussion of the nature of time in the chapter on the song "Time," which began with Jung seeing it as needing to be supplemented with the synchronicity factor, and continuing with Einstein, Jaynes, and Sartre, seeing it as an illusion or a nothingness. This would then suggest that a life can indeed be thought of as a panorama, as an unbroken vista which can be examined in every part, as opposed to a dwindling single bit of circumstance at the moment of death.

The final "Eclipse" lines that follow this list indicate that indeed for each life there is some kind of harmony within itself: *and everything under the sun is in tune.* Whatever way a life has been spent, these lines suggest, that life is complete within itself, and means exactly what the person living it has chosen it to mean. But that phrase is immediately followed by the line from which "Eclipse" gets its title: *But the sun is eclipsed by the moon.*

The implications of this final line are critical to the way the album finally expresses itself as a whole.

---

[268] Albert Camus, "The Stranger: Albert Camus," trans. Stuart Gilbert, Internet Archive (Million Books Project, January 1, 1967), https://archive.org/details/TheStranger, pp. 98-99.

In one interpretation, this is an unfortunate line, suggesting that however brightly one's life has shone, it is eclipsed by death. However true to themselves or to what degree they might have wallowed in bad faith, whatever were the circumstances of their lives, everyone dies. The sum of a life after it has been lived is nothing, the brightest sun is made dark. There is certainly support for such an interpretation, particularly in "Breathe" and "Time."

Alternatively, and perhaps equally unfortunately, a life may have been lived up to a certain point and mental illness may change fundamentally — that is, eclipse — how that life proceeds henceforth. This interpretation is not out of step with the only other places the moon is mentioned on *The Dark Side of the Moon*, in the darkest parts of "Brain Damage:"

> *And if your head explodes with dark forebodings too*
>
> *I'll see you on the dark side of the moon.*
>
> ...
>
> *And if the band you're in starts playing different tunes*
>
> *I'll see you on the dark side of the moon.*

In these lines, the moon is associated with craven fear and dissociation, which in turn are the products of mental illness. And while the majority of people may not be genetically prone to mental illness, there is nonetheless the possibility of accidents, natural disasters, war, toxins, drugs, or other triggers which can knock a person completely off the path that they had been traveling previously. As was the case with the interpretation of eclipse as death, an eclipse of mental illness can indeed bring darkness where there was light before.

Neither of these interpretations of the line feels right, however. Instead, there is the sense in which the eclipse draws a veil over the day to day, allowing you to see the otherwise hidden corona of the sun — a transcendence of the ordinary. What is suddenly manifest may have been there all the time, yet remained unseen until an extraordinary alignment of heaven and earth takes place.

Almost everyone has had a strange sensation that there were connections or machineries beyond their perception. Whether it was a moment of *déja vu*, some uprush of religious feeling, receiving a call from or running into someone you hadn't heard from in years but were just thinking about, an uncanny coincidence, or some other manifestation, the feeling of something outside the ordinary was palpable. Such feelings were well described more than 100 years ago by William James in his lecture on "The Reality of the Unseen," recorded in his book, *The Varieties of Religious Experience*:[269]

---

[269]William James, *The Varieties of Religious Experience*, p. 58 (emphasis original).

But the whole array of our instances leads to a conclusion something like this: It is as if there were in the human consciousness *a sense of reality, a feeling of objective presence, a perception* of what we may call "something there," more deep and more general than any of the special and particular "senses" by which the current psychology supposes existent realities to be originally revealed.

The eclipse is thus an experience of that "something there," to which James refers. James also describes the reality and power of such experiences:[270]

They are as convincing to those who have them as any direct sensible experiences can be, and they are, as a rule, much more convincing than results established by mere logic ever are. One may indeed be entirely without them; probably more than one of you here present is without them in any marked degree; but if you do have them, and have them at all strongly, the probability is that you cannot help regarding them as genuine perceptions of truth, as revelations of a kind of reality which no adverse argument, however unanswerable by you in words, can expel from your belief.

Once someone has experienced the eclipse and seen the corona, however briefly, there is no going back to the flatness of before. The awareness of something more never goes away. That seems much more the meaning of the line, *but the sun is eclipsed by the moon.*

As if to underscore the idea that there is more to the world than may meet the eye, "Eclipse" is not over when the singing has stopped, nor even when the organ's last note has faded. The very end of the album is like the footsteps after the crash in "On The Run," an escape from what had seemed inescapable.

What is left in "Eclipse" is the heartbeat again, with which the album began. A few seconds into this heartbeat comes a very distinct voice to say, *There is no dark side of the moon really. Matter of fact it's all dark.* This last voice is the same as one of the first heard at the beginning of the record, during "Speak To Me," saying *"I've always been mad, I know I've been mad, like the most of us are."*

The heartbeat continues for another twenty seconds before finally fading away, leaving the listener where he or she had begun, in silence.

---

[270] *Id.*, p. 72.

BIBLIOGRAPHY

Augustyn, Adam. "Chorus." *Encyclopædia Britannica.* Encyclopædia Britannica, Inc. Accessed November 23, 2020. https://www.britannica.com/art/chorus-theatre.

"Alan Parsons." GRAMMY.com, July 29, 2020. https://www.grammy.com/grammys/artists/alan-parsons/13857.

"Albert Camus Facts." NobelPrize.org. Nobel Media AB. Accessed November 22, 2020. https://www.nobelprize.org/prizes/literature/1957/camus/facts/.

Alden, Todd. Warhol and the Velvet Underground: Intermedia Collaborations 1966-67, 2014. http://www.aldenprojects.com/2014/11/warhol-and-velvet-underground.html.

Amadeo, Kimberly. "Deinstitutionalization, Its Causes, Effects, Pros and Cons: How Deinstitutionalization in the 1970s Affects You Today." The Balance. Dotdash, September 24, 2020. https://www.thebalance.com/deinstitutionalization-3306067.

Andrews, Robin. "Scientists Just Replicated The Infamous Milgram Experiment." IFLScience. IFLScience, March 17, 2017. https://www.iflscience.com/brain/scientists-replicated-infamous-milgram-experiment.

Aronson, Ronald. "Albert Camus." Stanford Encyclopedia of Philosophy. Stanford University, April 10, 2017. https://plato.stanford.edu/entries/camus/.

Baars, Bernard J. "The Global Workspace Theory of Consciousness." Wiley Online Library. John Wiley & Sons, Ltd, March 17, 2017. https://onlinelibrary.wiley.com/doi/10.1002/9781119132363.ch16.

Beatles Lyrics: The Fool on the Hill. BeatlesLyrics.org, 2008. https://www. beatleslyrics.org/index_files/Page7228.htm.

Bell, Chris, and Nk. "a List Obligatory. Songs about Time, Vol. 4: the Final Countdown." Earbuddy, July 24, 2013. https://www.earbuddy.net/7546/a-list-obligatory-songs-about-time-vol-4-the-final-countdown.html/columns.

Bellow, Saul. *Dangling Man.* New York: Signet, 1974. Available online at "Dangling Man." Internet Archive. Digital Library of India, September 22, 2015. https://archive.org/details/in.ernet.dli.2015.470139.

Bible Gateway. Accessed November 23, 2020. https://www.biblegateway.com.

Billboard Staff. "Roger Waters Revisits The 'Dark Side'." *Billboard*, January 10, 2013. https://www.billboard.com/articles/news/58519/roger-waters-revisits-the-dark-side.

Biography.com Editors. "Janis Joplin Biography." The Biography.com website. A&E Television Networks, April 4, 2014. https://www.biography.com/people/janis-joplin.

Blackgard, Cap. "What's in the Box!?: Pink Floyd - The Dark Side of the Moon Immersion Box Set." Consequence of Sound, January 16, 2014. http://consequenceofsound.net/2011/12/whats-in-the-box-pink-floyd-the-dark-side-of-the-moon-immersion-box-set.

Blagovest Bells. "What Is a Bell?" Blagovest Bells What is a bell? Blagovest Bells / Expanding Edge LLC. Accessed November 23, 2020. http://www.russianbells.com/acoustics/what-is-bell.html.

Blake, Mark. *Comfortably Numb: the inside Story of Pink Floyd.* Cambridge, MA: Da Capo Press, Perseus Books Group, 2008.

Blake, William. "Poetry And Prose Of William Blake." Edited by Geoffrey Keynes. Internet Archive. The Nonesuch Press, Bloomsbury, November 2, 2018. https://archive.org/details/dli.bengal.10689.21604.

Bourne, Mark. "The DVD Journal: Quick Reviews: I'm All Right Jack." The DVD Journal | Quick Reviews: I'm All Right Jack. The DVD Journal. Accessed November 20, 2020. http://www.dvdjournal.com/quickreviews/i/imallrightjack.q.shtml.

Broder, David S. "Nixon Wins Landslide Victory; Democrats Hold Senate, House McGovern Admits Defeat; President Calls for Harmony." *The Washington Post*. WP Company, November 8, 1972. http://www.washington-post.com/wp-srv/national/longterm/watergate/articles/110872-1.htm.

Brown, Jeremy. "Newsweek Special Edition: The Artists Behind Pink Floyd's Sound." *Newsweek*. Newsweek Digital LLC, June 8, 2015. https://www.newsweek.com/pink-floyd-sound-353897.

Camus, Albert. *The Myth of Sisyphus and Other Essays.* Translated by Justin O'Brien. New York: Vintage Books, 1955.

Camus, Albert. "The Stranger: Albert Camus." Translated by Stuart Gilbert. Internet Archive. Million Books Project, January 1, 1967. https://archive. org/details/TheStranger.

Carpenter, William T, and James I Koenig. "The Evolution of Drug Development in Schizophrenia: Past Issues and Future Opportunities." *Nature News.* Nature Publishing Group, November 28, 2007. https://www.nature. com/articles/1301639.

Caulfield, Keith. "Pink Floyd's 'Dark Side of the Moon' Sales Climb in Wake of Solar Eclipse." *Billboard,* August 22, 2017. https://www.billboard.com/ articles/columns/chart-beat/7940910/pink-floyd-dark-side-of-the-moon-solar-eclipse-sales.

Cavanagh, David. "The Glory and Torment of Being Syd Barrett, by David Bowie, David Gilmour, Mick Rock, Joe Boyd, Damon Albarn and More..." *UNCUT.* BandLab Technologies, January 24, 2014. http://www. uncut.co.uk/features/the-glory-and-torment-of-being-syd-barrett-by-david-bowie-david-gilmour-mick-rock-joe-boyd-damon-albarn-and-more-13127.

Cavanna, Andrea Eugenio, Michael Trimble, Frederico Cinti, and Francesco Monaco. "The 'Bicameral Mind' 30 Years on: a Critical Reappraisal of Julian Jaynes' Hypothesis." *Functional Neurology.* U.S. National Library of Medicine, 2007. https://pubmed.ncbi.nlm.nih.gov/17509238.

Chadwick, David R. "A Profile of the San Francisco Zen Center." Crooked Cucumber, April 2002. http://www.cuke.com/dchad/writ/short/sfzc%20 profile.html.

Cherry, Kendra. "The Life and Theories of Psychologist William James." Verywell Mind. Dotdash, April 23, 2020. http://psychology.about.com/od/ profilesofmajorthinkers/p/jamesbio.htm.

Child, June. "Life with Syd Barrett." Bolan World, June 8, 2017. https:// mistymist.wordpress.com/discography/ride-a-white-swan/june-child/.

Chorus America. "The Mikado, The Collegiate Chorale, Carnegie Hall." The Mikado | Chorus America. Chorus America, April 2012. https://www. chorusamerica.org/calendar/mikado.

Cirigliano II, Michael. "Hokusai and Debussy's Evocations of the Sea." metmuseum.org, July 22, 2014. http://www.metmuseum.org/blogs/now-at-the-met/2014/debussy-la-mer.

Classic Album Sundays. "The Story of Lou Reed 'Transformer'." Classic Album Sundays, December 29, 2018. https://classicalbumsundays.com/album-of-the-month-lou-reed-transformer.

Clayton, Merry. "Merry Clayton - Gimme Shelter." Internet Archive, September 1, 2011. https://archive.org/details/MerryClayton-GimmeShelter.

Cossar, Neil. "The Great Gig In The Sky." This Day In Music, March 4, 2020. https://www.thisdayinmusic.com/liner-notes/the-great-gig-in-the-sky.

De Laurence, Lauron William. "The Illustrated Key to the Tarot: The Veil of Divination." Internet Archive. Project Gutenberg, August 1, 2018. https://archive.org/details/theillustratedke43548gut.

"Debussy: La Mer." *The Guardian.* Guardian News and Media, March 3, 2000. https://www.theguardian.com/culture/2000/mar/03/classicalmusicandopera.

Deutsch, Mark. Clare Torry: Her greatest gig. The one she almost skipped., January 1, 1970. http://markdeutsch39.blogspot.com/2013/03/clare-torry-her-greatest-gig-one-she.html.

Dill, Ann E. P. *Managing to Care: Case Management and Service System Reform.* New York: Aldine de Gruyter, 2001.

Diltz, Henry. "Keith Richards and Ron Wood, Los Angeles, CA, 1979." Keith Richards and Ronnie Wood on Lear Jet (1979). Accessed November 23, 2020. https://www.morrisonhotelgallery.com/photographs/cl9oZa/Keith-Richards-and-Ron-Wood-Los-Angeles-CA-1979.

Dowling, Stephen. "Banned: The Songs Deemed 'Too Dangerous' for the BBC." BBC Culture. BBC, June 20, 2019. http://www.bbc.com/culture/story/20190620-banned-the-songs-deemed-too-dangerous-for-the-bbc.

Einstein, Albert, and Stephen Hawking. *A Stubbornly Persistent Illusion: the Essential Scientific Writings of Albert Einstein.* Philadelphia: Running Press, 2009.

El-Rahman, Minara. "The Final Cut: Pink Floyd and EMI Group Lawsuit." Findlaw, March 21, 2019. https://blogs.findlaw.com/decided/2010/03/the-final-cut-pink-floyd-and-emi-group-lawsuit.html.

Eliot, T. S. "Prufrock and Other Observations." Internet Archive. The Egoist Ltd., University of California Libraries, November 17, 2006. https://archive.org/details/prufrockandother00eliorich.

Eliot, T. S. "The Waste Land, 1922 First Edition of the Book and Poem by T. S. Eliot." Edited by Wikisource contributors. Wikisource, the free online library. Wikimedia Foundation, Inc., July 19, 2018. https://en.wikisource.org/w/index.php?title=The_Waste_Land.

Encina, Gregorio Billikopf. Milgram's Experiment on Obedience to Authority. The Regents of the University of California, November 15, 2004. https://nature.berkeley.edu/ucce50/ag-labor/7article/article35.htm.

Erickson, Glenn. "THE Peter Sellers Collection." DVD Savant Review: The Peter Sellers Collection. MH Sub I, LLC dba Internet Brands, March 3, 2003. http://www.dvdsavant.com/s744sell.html.

Eschner, Kat. "The Bowdlers Wanted to Clean Up Shakespeare, Not Become a Byword for Censorship." Smithsonian.com. Smithsonian Institution, July 11, 2017. https://www.smithsonianmag.com/smart-news/bowdlers-wanted-clean-shakespeare-not-become-byword-censorship-180963945.

Falk, Dan, and Quanta. "The Debate Over Time's Place in the Universe." *The Atlantic*. Atlantic Media Company, July 26, 2016. https://www.theatlantic.com/science/archive/2016/07/the-debate-over-times-place-in-the-universe/492464/.

Far Out Staff. "Hear Pink Floyd Gem 'Money' through Roger Waters' Isolated Bass Track." *Far Out Magazine*, August 7, 2020. https://faroutmagazine.co.uk/roger-waters-pink-floyd-money-isolated-bass-track.

"Film in 1960." Film in 1960 | BAFTA Awards. British Academy of Film and Television Arts. Accessed November 23, 2020. http://awards.bafta.org/award/1960/film.

Flood, Alison. "Jean-Paul Sartre Rejected Nobel Prize in a Letter to Jury That Arrived Too Late." *The Guardian*. Guardian News and Media, January 5, 2015. https://www.theguardian.com/books/2015/jan/05/sartre-nobel-prize-literature-letter-swedish-academy.

Force, James E., and Sarah Hutton. *Newton and Newtonianism: New Studies*. Dordrecht: Kluwer Academic Publishers, 2004.

Fortescue-Brickdale, Eleanor, ed. "The Book of Old English Songs and Ballads." Internet Archive. Hodder and Stoughton, University of California Libraries, December 14, 2007. https://archive.org/details/bookofoldenglish00fortrich.

Freeman, Walter, and James W Watts. "Prefrontal Lobotomy: The Surgical Relief of Mental Pain." National Center for Biotechnology Information. U.S. National Library of Medicine, October 22, 1942. https://www.ncbi.nlm.nih.gov/pmc/articles/PMC1933933/pdf/bullnyacadmed00561-0025.pdf.

Fusar-Poli, Paolo, and Pierluigi Politi. "Paul Eugen Bleuler and the Birth of Schizophrenia (1908)." *The American Journal of Psychiatry*. U.S. National Library of Medicine, November 2008. http://www.ncbi.nlm.nih.gov/pubmed/18981075.

Gallucci, Ennio. "Who Sang the Most Pink Floyd Songs? Lead Vocal Totals." Ultimate Classic Rock. Ultimate Classic Rock, June 16, 2020. https://ultimateclassicrock.com/pink-floyd-lead-vocals-songs.

Gilbert, William Schwenck, and Arthur Sullivan. "An Entirely Original Supernatural Opera,: in Two Acts,: Entitled: Ruddigore;: or,: The Witche's Curse! : Sullivan, Arthur, 1842-1900, Composer; Gilbert, William Schwenck, 1836-1911, Librettist." Internet Archive. London: Chappell, Harold B. Lee Library, Brigham Young University, January 1, 1887. https://archive.org/details/entirelyoriginal1887sull.

Gilbert, William Schwenck, and Arthur Sullivan. Full text of "The Mikado Or The Town Of Titipu". Universal Digital Library, July 1, 2004. https://archive.org/stream/mikadoorthetowno002227mbp/mikadoorthetowno002227mbp_djvu.txt.

Gillan, Ian. "Ian Comments on the Words of Some Songs in His Life - 16 'Child in Time'." Caramba!-Wordography. Accessed November 23, 2020. http://www.gillan.com/wordography-16.html.

"Glossary of Roman Catholic Church Terms, Words and Phrases." CatholicIreland.net. The Church Support Group). Accessed November 23, 2020. https://www.catholicireland.net/glossary-of-terms.

Goodden, Joe. "Maharishi Mahesh Yogi." The Beatles Bible, June 8, 2020. https://www.beatlesbible.com/people/maharishi-mahesh-yogi.

Goodman, Elizabeth. "Jim Morrison's Death May Be Reinvestigated." *Rolling Stone*. Penske Business Media, LLC., June 25, 2018. https://www.rollingstone.com/music/news/jim-morrisons-death-may-be-reinvestigated-20070710.

Grant, Michael. "Horace." *Encyclopædia Britannica*. Encyclopædia Britannica, Inc. Accessed November 20, 2020. https://www.britannica.com/biography/Horace-Roman-poet.

Graves, Robert. *Goodbye to All That*. London: Folio Society, 1981.

Havers, Richard. "The Successful Launch Of Apple Records: UDiscover." uDiscover Music, August 26, 2020. https://www.udiscovermusic.com/stories/d-day-for-apple-records.

Heckers, Stephan. "Bleuler and the Neurobiology of Schizophrenia." *Schizophrenia Bulletin*. Oxford University Press, November 2011. https://www.ncbi.nlm.nih.gov/pmc/articles/PMC3196934.

Hilton, James. *Lost Horizons*. New York: HarperCollins, 2012.

History.com Editors. "Industrial Revolution." History.com. A&E Television Networks, September 9, 2019. https://www.history.com/topics/industrial-revolution/industrial-revolution.

History.com Editors. "V-J Day." History.com. A&E Television Networks, October 14, 2009. https://www.history.com/topics/world-war-ii/v-j-day.

Homer. *The Iliad*. Translated by Robert Fagles. New York: Penguin, 1990.

Horace. "The Satires, Epistles, and Art of Poetry of Horace, Tr. into Engl. Verse by John Conington: Quintus Horatius Flaccus." Translated by John Conington. Internet Archive. Oxford University, January 3, 2010. https://archive.org/details/satiresepistles00flacgoog.

HyperWar Foundation. *HyperWar: Royal Air Force 1939–1945: Volume I: The Fight at Odds* [Chapter VII]. Accessed November 20, 2020. http://www.ibiblio.org/hyperwar/UN/UK/UK-RAF-I/UK-RAF-I-7.html.

"Introducing Newton's Alchemical Papers." The Newton Project. Accessed November 23, 2020. http://www.newtonproject.ox.ac.uk/texts/newtons-works/alchemical.

"Jakob Böhme." Jakob Böhme - New World Encyclopedia. Paragon House Publishers. Accessed November 23, 2020. https://www.newworldency-clopedia.org/entry/Jakob_B%C3%B6hme.

James, William, and Reinhold Niebuhr. *The Varieties of Religious Experience: a Study in Human Nature ; with a New Introd. by Reinhold Niebuhr*. New York: Simon & Schuster, 1997.

James, William. "The Principles of Psychology, Vol. I and II." Internet Archive. H. Holt, January 1, 1890. https://archive.org/details/principlespsych-01jamegoog/page/n4/mode/2up, /n6/mode/2up.

Jansson, Bengt. "Controversial Psychosurgery Resulted in a Nobel Prize." NobelPrize.org. Nobel Media AB, October 29, 1998. https://www.nobel-prize.org/nobel_prizes/medicine/laureates/1949/moniz-article.html.

Jaynes, Julian. *The Origin of Consciousness in the Breakdown of the Bicameral Mind*. Boston: Houghton Mifflin Company, 1976.

"Jean-Paul Sartre Documentary." NobelPrize.org. Nobel Media AB. Accessed November 22, 2020. https://www.nobelprize.org/prizes/literature/1964/sartre/documentary.

Jones, Sam. "Pink Floyd and EMI Agree Deal Allowing Sale of Single Digital Downloads." *The Guardian*. Guardian News and Media, January 4, 2011. https://www.theguardian.com/music/2011/jan/04/pink-floyd-emi-single-digital-downloads.

Joshua. "History of Private Jets, Planes & Aviation." Charter Jet One. Charter Jet One, August 9, 2020. https://charterjetone.com/history-of-private-jets-aviation.

Jung, Carl G. *The Collected Works of C.G. Jung: The Archetypes and the Collective Unconscious.* Edited by Gerhard Adler, Herbert Read, and Michael Fordham. Translated by Richard Francis Carrington. Hull. 2nd ed. London: Routledge & Kegen Paul, 1969.

Jung, Carl G. and Richard Wilhelm. *The Secret of the Golden Flower, a Chinese Book of Life, Translated and Explained by Richard Wilhelm, with an European Commentary by C.G. Jung.* Translated by Richard Wilhelm. London: Kegan Paul, Trench, Trubner and C°, 1947

Jung, Carl G., Marie-Luise von Franz, Joseph L. Henderson, Jolande Jacobi, and Aniela Jaffé. *Man and His Symbols.* New York: Dell Pub. Co., 1964.

Jung, Carl G. *Synchronicity: an Acausal Connecting Principle.* Edited by Michael Fordham. Translated by Richard Francis Carrington Hull. Princeton: Princeton University Press, 1973.

Jung, Carl. "C. G. Jung Collected Works Vol 7 Part 1 The Effects Of The Unconscious Upon Consciousness." Internet Archive, January 1, 1966. https://archive.org/details/C.G.JungCollectedWorksVol7Part1TheEffectsOfThe UnconsciousUponConsciousness.

Jung, Carl. "C. G. Jung Collected Works: Vol 7, Part 2: Individuation." Internet Archive, January 1, 1966. https://archive.org/details/C.G.JungCollectedW orksVol7Part2Individuation/page/n9/mode/2u.

Jung, Carl. *Memories, Dreams, Reflections.* Revised ed., recorded and edited by Aniela Jaffe, translated by Richard and Clara Winston, New York: Random House, 1965.

Kendall, Charlie. "From the Source, with Host Charlie Kendall - Interview with David Gilmour." The Source. The Pink Floyd Fan Club, April 6, 1984. http://www.pink-floyd.org/artint/28.htm.

Kerouac, Jack. *On the Road.* New York: Penguin, 2016.

Kerouac, Jack. *The Dharma Bums.* New York: Viking Press, 1971.

Kierkegaard, Søren. "Fear-and-Trembling-Johannes-De-Silentio." Translated by Walter Lowrie. Internet Archive. Siegfried, July 5, 2015. https://archive. org/details/fear-and-trembling-johannes-de-silentio.

Kierkegaard, Søren. *Kierkegaard's Attack upon "Christendom": 1848-1855.* Translated by Walter Lowrie. Boston: The Beacon Press, 1960.

Kierkegaard, Søren. "Three Discourses On Imagined Occasions." Internet Archive. Digital Library of India, January 1, 1970. https://archive.org/ details/in.ernet.dli.2015.504972/page/n99/mode/2up.

Kitchen, Matthew. "What Is Pink Floyd's Dark Side of the Moon Really About? An Introduction." *Esquire,* August 22, 2020. https://www.esquire.

com/entertainment/music/a17945/what-is-dark-side-of-the-moon-about-15266894.

Koestler, Arthur. *The Ghost in the Machine*. London: Arkana, 1989.

Kreps, Daniel. "Carly Simon Refutes Theory That 'So Vain' Target Is David Geffen." *Rolling Stone*. Rolling Stone, May 29, 2020. https://www.rollingstone.com/music/music-news/carly-simon-refutes-theory-that-so-vain-target-is-david-geffen-102891.

Krishan, Gaurav. "21 Musicians and the Football Clubs They Support," February 11, 2017. https://www.sportskeeda.com/football/21-musicians-football-clubs-they-support/11.

Kuijsten, Marcel. "Ten Questions Critics Fail to Answer About Julian Jaynes's Theory." Julian Jaynes Society, October 28, 2019. https://www.julianjaynes.org/blog/julian-jaynes-theory/ten-questions-critics-fail-to-answer-about-julian-jayness-theory.

Lake, Greg. "Lucky Man by Emerson, Lake & Palmer." Songfacts. Songfacts, LLC. Accessed November 23, 2020. https://www.songfacts.com/lyrics/emerson-lake-palmer/lucky-man.

Lamb, Charles, and Mary Lamb. *Tales from Shakespeare*. Illustr. Louis Rhead. New York: Harper & Bros., 1918. Available online at "Tales from Shakespeare." Internet Archive. Harper & Bros, New York, London/University of North Carolina at Chapel Hill, March 19, 2012. https://archive.org/details/talesfromshakesplamb.

Lawrence, D. H. "Sons and Lovers." Internet Archive. Mitchell Kennerley, New York, September 5, 2015. https://archive.org/details/lawrence_d_h_1885_1930_sons_and_lovers.

Lawrence, David Herbert. "Lady Chatterley's Lover." Internet Archive. Digital Library of India, June 25, 2015. https://archive.org/details/in.ernet.dli.2015.38592.

Lennon, John, and Paul McCartney. "I Am the Walrus (Lennon-McCartney)." Beatles Lyrics: I am the Walrus. Accessed November 23, 2020. https://www.beatleslyrics.org/index_files/Page7413.htm.

Lewis, Tanya. "Lobotomy: Definition, Procedure & History." LiveScience. Future US, Inc., August 29, 2014. https://www.livescience.com/42199-lobotomy-definition.html.

Libet Experiments. The Information Philosopher. Accessed November 22, 2020. http://informationphilosopher.com/freedom/libet_experiments.html.

Lifton, Dave. "Alan Wilson of Canned Heat Rockers Who Died at Age 27." Ultimate Classic Rock. Townsquare Media, Inc., August 22, 2013. https://ultimateclassicrock.com/alan-wilson-rockers-who-died-at-age-27.

Lifton, Dave. "When the Beatles Cleaned Out Their Closet for the 'Hey Jude' LP." Ultimate Classic Rock. Ultimate Classic Rock, February 25, 2020. https://ultimateclassicrock.com/beatles-hey-jude-album.

Lorentz, H. A., Albert Einstein, H. Minkowski, and H. Weyl. "The Principle of Relativity. Memoirs on the Special and General Theory of Relativity." Edited by A. Sommerfeld. Translated by W. Perrett and G. B. Jeffery. Internet Archive. Dover, October 11, 2013. https://archive.org/details/principlerelativ00halo/page/n69/mode/2up.

Luebering, J. E. "Thomas Bowdler." *Encyclopædia Britannica*. Encyclopædia Britannica, inc. Accessed November 22, 2020. https://www.britannica.com/biography/Thomas-Bowdler.

Maasik, Sonia, and Jack Solomon, eds. *Signs of Life in the USA: Readings on Popular Culture for Writers*. Boston: Bedford/St Martins, 2011.

"Map of Total Solar Eclipse on March 7, 1970." timeanddate.com. Time and Date AS. Accessed November 23, 2020. https://www.timeanddate.com/eclipse/map/1970-march-7.

Marcuse, Herbert. *Eros and Civilization: A Philosophical Inquiry into Freud*. Boston: Beacon Press, 1955.

Martin, Gary. "'Hobson's Choice' - the Meaning and Origin of This Phrase." Phrasefinder. Accessed November 20, 2020. https://www.phrases.org.uk/meanings/hobsons-choice.html.

Matthiessen, Peter. *The Snow Leopard*. New York: Bantam Books, 1979.

McCue, Jim, and Christopher Ricks. "Masterpiece in the Making - Poetry." TLS. The Times Literary Supplement Limited, November 2015. https://www.the-tls.co.uk/articles/masterpiece-in-the-making.

McDonald, William. "Søren Kierkegaard." *Stanford Encyclopedia of Philosophy*. Stanford University, November 10, 2017. https://plato.stanford.edu/entries/kierkegaard/.

Mcleod, Saul. "The Milgram Shock Experiment." Milgram Experiment | Simply Psychology. Accessed November 20, 2020. https://www.simplypsychology.org/milgram.html.

Milgram, Stanley. "The Perils of Obedience." *Harper's Magazine* 247, no. 1483, December 1973.

MOJO Staff. "MOJO Issue 193 / December 2009." *Mojo.* Bauer Media Group, December 17, 2009. https://www.mojo4music.com/articles/2420/mojo-issue-193-december-2009.

Mora, J. J. "Reynard the Fox." Internet Archive. Boston, D. Estes & Co, January 1, 1970. https://archive.org/details/reynardfox00unse/page/n12/mode/1up.

More, Thomas. *Utopia.* New York, NY: Penguin Books, 2012.

Moreton, Cole. "Roger Waters: Backstage as He Prepares for The Wall Live Show." Daily Mail Online. Associated Newspapers, November 7, 2010. https://www.dailymail.co.uk/home/moslive/article-1327045/Roger-Waters-Backstage-prepares-The-Wall-live-show.html.

Nichols, Sallie. *Jung and Tarot: An Archetypal Journey.* Boston: Red Wheel/Weiser, LLC, 1980.

Nobel Lectures: Physics: 1942-1962. Amsterdam: Published for the Nobel Foundation by Elsevier, 1964.

NPR Staff. "Mick Jagger On The Apocalyptic 'Gimme Shelter'." NPR. NPR, November 16, 2012. https://www.npr.org/2012/11/16/165270769/mick-jagger-on-the-apocalyptic-gimme-shelter.

O'Bannon, Kathleen. "Jacob Behmen, An Appreciation, by Alexander Whyte." Christian Classics Ethereal Library. Harry Plantinga. Accessed November 23, 2020. https://www.ccel.org/ccel/whyte/behmen.html.

O'Brien, Andrew. "Remembering The Troubled Genius Of Syd Barrett On 'The Piper At The Gates Of Dawn'." L4LM, January 6, 2020. https://liveforlivemusic.com/features/pink-floyd-piper-gates-dawn-1967.

Orwell, George. *1984.* New York: Signet, 1983.

Orwell, George. Full text of "DOWN AND OUT IN PARIS AND LONDON - ENGLISH - GEORGE ORWELL". The University of Adelaide Library, May 14, 2004. https://archive.org/stream/DownAndOutInParisAndLondon-English-GeorgeOrwell/orwellparislondon_djvu.txt.

"Past Leadership." theASSC.org. Association For The Scientific Study Of Consciousness, 2020. https://theassc.org/past-leadership.

Perna, Alan Di, Jeff Kitts, and Brad Tolinski. *Guitar World Presents Pink Floyd.* Milwaukee, WI: Hal Leonard, 2002.

Petridis, Alexis. "Obituary: Gus Dudgeon." *The Guardian.* Guardian News and Media, July 23, 2002. https://www.theguardian.com/news/2002/jul/23/guardianobituaries.alexispetridis.

"Pink Floyd - Crackers (Damn Braces: Bless Relaxes) The Entire 1972 Hollywood Bowl Concert." Discogs, January 1, 1976. https://www.discogs.com/

Pink-Floyd-Crackers-Damn-Braces-Bless-Relaxes-The-Entire-1972-Hollywood-Bowl-Concert/release/1135332.

Pink Floyd. "Fearless Lyrics." Fearless lyrics - Meddle Lyrics - Pink Floyd Lyrics, November 2020. http://www.pink-floyd-lyrics.com/html/fearless-meddle-lyrics.html.

Pink Floyd. "Pink Floyd Live March 13, 1972." Internet Archive, March 16, 2014. https://archive.org/details/pf_1972-03-13_04/REC 1 - Brain Damage unedited.flac.

Pink Floyd. *The Dark Side of the Moon: Immersion Box Set.* Capitol Records, 2011.

"Pink Floyd." This Day In Music, February 2, 2020. https://www.thisdayinmusic.com/artists/pink-floyd.

"Pink Floyd: The Official Site." Pink Floyd | The Official Site. Accessed November 22, 2020. https://www.pinkfloyd.com/history/timeline_1973.php, /timeline_1974.php.

Pirsig, Robert. *Zen and the Art of Motorcycle Maintenance.* New York: Random House, 1984.

Poe, Edgar Allan. "The Bells." Internet Archive. Philadelphia, Porter & Coates/Library of Congress, November 18, 2010. https://archive.org/details/bells00poee.

Prideaux, Ed. "You Feel Me: Syd Barrett and The Madcap Laughs." *Cultural Weekly*. Next Echo Foundation, July 11, 2018. https://www.culturalweekly.com/feel-syd-barrett-madcap-laughs.

Rae, Kit. Dark Side of the Moon Mp3 Soundclips. Accessed November 22, 2020. http://www.kitrae.net/music/Music_mp3_DSOTM_3.html.

Reginald, Reginald. "Billy Dolls Murcia (1951-1972) - Find A Grave..." Find a Grave. Ancestry, July 21, 2006. https://www.findagrave.com/memorial/15004578/billy-dolls-murcia.

Reising, Russell. *Speak to Me: the Legacy of Pink Floyd's The Dark Side of the Moon.* Aldershot: Ashgate, 2005.

Richards, Keith, and Mick Jagger. "Happy by The Rolling Stones." Songfacts. Sony/ATV Music Publishing LLC. Accessed November 23, 2020. https://www.songfacts.com/lyrics/the-rolling-stones/happy.

Ripley, Sherman, ed. "Beyond : an Anthology of Immortality." Internet Archive. D. Appleton and Company, New York / State Library of Pennsylvania, January 1, 1970. https://archive.org/details/beyondanthologyo00unse.

Robertson, Geoffrey. "The Trial of Lady Chatterley's Lover." *The Guardian*. Guardian News and Media, October 22, 2010. https://www.theguardian.com/books/2010/oct/22/dh-lawrence-lady-chatterley-trial.

Robinson, Edwin Arlington. "Richard Cory by Edwin Arlington Robinson." Poetry Foundation. Poetry Foundation. Accessed November 23, 2020. https://www.poetryfoundation.org/poems/44982/richard-cory.

"Roger & Me." IMDb. IMDb.com. Accessed November 23, 2020. https://www.imdb.com/title/tt0098213/plotsummary?ref_=tt_stry_pl.

Rolling Stone. "Alan Parsons on 'Dark Side': 'Roger Knew Something Great Was in the Making'." *Rolling Stone.* Rolling Stone, June 25, 2018. https://www.rollingstone.com/music/news/alan-parsons-on-dark-side-roger-knew-something-great-was-in-the-making-20110928.

Rolling Stone. "Hendrix Inquest Inconclusive Not Enough Evidence to Say for Sure What Motives Were behind Jimi's Death." *Rolling Stone.* Penske Business Media, LLC, June 25, 2018. https://www.rollingstone.com/music/news/hendrix-inquest-inconclusive-19701029.

Romm, Cari. "Rethinking One of Psychology's Most Infamous Experiments." *The Atlantic.* Atlantic Media Company, January 28, 2015. https://www.theatlantic.com/health/archive/2015/01/rethinking-one-of-psychologys-most-infamous-experiments/384913/.

Rothman, David J. *The Discovery of the Asylum: Social Order and Disorder in the New Republic.* London: Routledge, 2017.

Salvan Jacques Léon, and Ita Kanter. *To Be and Not to Be an Analysis of Jean-Paul Sartre's Ontology.* Detroit: Wayne State University Press, 1962.

"Sartre Awarded Nobel Prize, but Rejects It; Existentialist Thinks His Writings Would. Be Compromised; $53,000 Will Revert to Fund, Swedish Academy Says." *The New York Times.* The New York Times Company, October 23, 1964. https://www.nytimes.com/1964/10/23/archives/sartre-awarded-nobel-prize-but-rejects-it-existentialist-thinks-his.html.

Sartre, Jean-Paul. *Being and Nothingness: an Essay on Phenomenological Ontology.* Translated by Hazel E. Barnes. New York: Philosophical Library, 1966.

Sartre, Jean-Paul. *Existentialism and Humanism.* Translated by Philip Mairet. London: Methuen, 1948.

Sartre, Jean-Paul. *No Exit and Three Other Plays.* New York: Vintage Books, 1955. Online at Internet Archive, October 7, 2011. https://archive.org/details/NoExit.

Sartre, Jean-Paul. *The Age of Reason.* Translated by Eric Sutton. London: Random House, 1947.

Sartre, Jean-Paul. "[Jean Paul Sartre] Existentialism Is A Humanism (z Lib. org)." Edited by John Kulka. Translated by Carol Macomber. Internet Archive. Yale University Press, December 20, 2019. https://archive.org/details/jeanpaulsartreexistentialismisahumanismzlib.org.

Schedneck, Brooke. "Thich Nhat Hanh, the Buddhist Monk Who Introduced Mindfulness to the West, Prepares to Die." The Conversation, June 4, 2020. https://theconversation.com/thich-nhat-hanh-the-buddhist-monk-who-introduced-mindfulness-to-the-west-prepares-to-die-111142.

Schäfer, Tom. "Nick Mason: Der Rhythmusarchitekt Von Pink Floyd." *STICKS*, May 7, 2019. https://www.sticks.de/stories/nick-mason-der-rhythmusar-chitekt-von-pink-floyd.

Shakespeare, William. *The Yale Shakespeare*. Edited by Tucker Brooke and Wilbur L. Cross. New York: Barnes & Noble, 1993.

Shane III, Leo. "Number of Homeless Vets Rises for First Time in Seven Years." *Military Times*. Sightline Media Group, December 6, 2017. https://www.militarytimes.com/veterans/2017/12/06/number-of-homeless-veterans-nationwide-rises-for-first-time-in-seven-years.

Simon, Carly. "You're So Vain by Carly Simon." Songfacts. Universal Music Publishing Group. Accessed November 23, 2020. https://www.songfacts.com/facts/carly-simon/youre-so-vain.

Simon, Paul. "Richard Cory." The Paul Simon Official Site, February 1, 2016. https://www.paulsimon.com/song/richard-cory.

"Sir Isaac Newton: Magician's Brain." *The Economist*. The Economist Newspaper, June 19, 2014. https://www.economist.com/books-and-arts/2014/06/19/magicians-brain.

"Sisyphus." Encyclopaedia Britannica, revised and updated by Jeff Wallenfeldt. *Encyclopædia Britannica*. Encyclopædia Britannica, Inc., Accessed July 10, 2020), https://www.britannica.com/topic/Sisyphus.

Squires, Nick. "Roger Waters Memorialises His Fallen WWII Father." *The Telegraph*. Telegraph Media Group, February 18, 2014. https://www.telegraph.co.uk/news/worldnews/europe/italy/10646870/Roger-Waters-memorialises-his-fallen-WWII-father.html.

Srivastava, S. P., and R. A. Folinsbee. "Measurement of Variations in the Total Geomagnetic Field at Sea off Nova Scotia." *Canadian Journal of Earth Sciences*. Canadian Science Publishing, February 1, 1975. https://cdnsciencepub.com/doi/10.1139/e75-020.

Stevens, Anthony. *Archetype Revisited: an Updated Natural History of the Self*. London: Brunner-Routledge, 2002.

Stone, Greg. "Why Camus Was Not An Existentialist." *Philosophy Now: a magazine of ideas*. Philosophy Now, 2016. https://philosophynow.org/issues/115/Why_Camus_Was_Not_An_Existentialist.

Styron, William. *Darkness Visible*. New York: Random House, 1992.

Suzuki Shunryū. *Zen Mind, Beginner's Mind: Informal Talks on Zen Meditation and Practice*. Boston, MA: Shambhala, 2011.

"The Nobel Prize in Literature 1976." NobelPrize.org. Nobel Media AB. Accessed December 28, 2020. https://www.nobelprize.org/prizes/literature/1976/summary

The Teaching of Buddha. Tokyo, Japan: Bukkyo Dendo Kyokai, 2002.

Teeter, R. M. "Memo; R. M. Teeter to H. R. Haldeman; Undated, but Ca. November 8, 1972; Folder 40-05-H.R. Haldeman; Box 40; Folder 5; Contested Materials Collection." Richard Nixon Presidential Library. National Archives, November 1972. https://www.nixonlibrary.gov/sites/default/files/virtuallibrary/documents/contested/contested_box_40/Contested-40-05.pdf.

Thoreau, Henry David. *Walden; or, Life in the Woods, and On the Duty of Civil Disobedience*. New York: Signet, 1963. Available online at "Walden; or, Life in the Woods." Internet Archive. Boston Public Library (Rare Books Department), Ticknor and Fields, January 1, 1970. https://archive.org/details/waldenorlifeinwo1854thor.

Tirosh, Gur. "The Complete True Story Behind 'American Pie' by Don McLean." History by day. History by Day, October 7, 2019. https://www.historybyday.com/human-stories/the-complete-true-story-behind-american-pie-by-don-mclean/.

Trueman, C N. "Coal Mines in the Industrial Revolution." History Learning Site, March 31, 2015. https://www.historylearningsite.co.uk/britain-1700-to-1900/industrial-revolution/coal-mines-in-the-industrial-revolution/.

Unterberger, Andrew. "10 Reasons Peter Gabriel's 'Solsbury Hill' Is One of the Greatest Songs of All Time." *Billboard*, March 11, 2018. https://www.billboard.com/articles/columns/rock/7702117/peter-gabriel-solsbury-hill-anniversary-greatest-song.

Updike, John. *Rabbit Redux*. New York: Penguin, 1973.

Updike, John. *Rabbit, Run*. New York: Fawcett Crest, 1983.

Venning, Thomas. "Time's Arrow: Albert Einstein's Letters to Michele Besso: Christie's." Einstein's letters to Michele Besso. Christie's, November 14, 2017. https://www.christies.com/features/Einstein-letters-to-Michele-Besso-8422-1.aspx.

Wawzenek, Bryan. "Pink Floyd's 'The Dark Side of the Moon': A Track-by-Track Guide." Ultimate Classic Rock. Ultimate Classic Rock, March 1, 2018. https://ultimateclassicrock.com/dark-side-of-the-moon-track-by-track/.

Wawzenek, Bryan. "When Pink Floyd Flubbed Live Debut of 'The Dark Side of the Moon'." Ultimate Classic Rock. Ultimate Classic Rock, March 2, 2018. http://ultimateclassicrock.com/pink-floyd-live-debut-dark-side.

Wegner, Daniel M., and Kurt Gray. *The Mind Club Who Thinks, What Feels, and Why It Matters*. New York, NY: Penguin Books, 2017.

"Yijing." *Encyclopædia Britannica*. Encyclopædia Britannica, Inc. Accessed November 23, 2020. https://www.britannica.com/topic/Yijing.

Zimbardo, Philip G. "2. Setting Up." Stanford Prison Experiment. Social Psychology Network, 1999. https://www.prisonexp.org/setting-up.

Printed in the United States
by Baker & Taylor Publisher Services